£3

*Never On O*

'The great appear greater because we are on are knees.
Let us rise.'

James Larkin

# Never On Our Knees
## A History of the RMT, 1979–2006

### MIKE BERLIN

Pluto  Press

LONDON • ANN ARBOR, MI

in association with the

NATIONAL UNION OF RAIL MARITIME AND TRANSPORT WORKERS

First published 2006 by Pluto Press
345 Archway Road, London N6 5AA
and 839 Greene Street, Ann Arbor, MI 48106

www.plutobooks.com

British Library Cataloguing in Publication Data
A catalogue record for this book is available from the British Library

ISBN   0 7453 2605 6 paperback

Library of Congress Cataloging in Publication Data applied for


10   9   8   7   6   5   4   3   2   1


Designed and produced for Pluto Press by
Chase Publishing Services Ltd, Fortescue, Sidmouth, EX10 9QG, England
Typeset from disk by Stanford DTP Services, Northampton, England
Printed and bound in the European Union by
Antony Rowe Ltd, Chippenham and Eastbourne, England

*This book is dedicated to
the memory of members of the RMT who have
died as a result of work related accidents
and illnesses in the last thirty years.*

# Contents

# List of Illustrations

# Preface

The National Union of Rail, Maritime and Transport Workers (RMT) has been at the forefront of industrial trade unionism in Britain for over a century. This book recounts the history of the union since 1979, a period of upheaval that has witnessed the privatisation of Britain's railways, the decimation of its merchant shipping fleet and the implementation of a raft of legislation aimed at destroying the rights of workers to collectively organise.

Formed in 1990 as a result of an amalgamation of the National Union of Seamen and the National Union of Railwaymen, the union traces its roots back to the era of 'All Industry' trade unions formed at the beginning of the twentieth century to unite skilled and unskilled workers in powerful blocs of organised labour. The RMT's predecessor union, the ASRS, was a prime mover in the formation of the Labour Party and has been central to the collective quest for social justice in modern Britain.

Throughout the 1980s and 1990s the union and its forerunners battled against the onslaughts against the trade union movement by the Thatcher government and resisted the continuation of many of these policies under New Labour. During this period members of the union also helped to sustain a sister union during the last years of Apartheid South Africa. Despite the folly of rail privatisation and the destruction of much of Britain's maritime capacity the RMT has rebuilt itself as a dynamic campaigning trade union, one of the fastest growing in Britain today.

This book chronicles the story of the last 27 years of industrial campaigning; the struggles against the decline of the shipping fleet and the privatisation of the railways, the fraught relationship with New Labour led by Tony Blair and the grass roots origins of today's activist resurgence.

# Author's Note and Acknowlegements

This book relates the history of the RMT over the past quarter of a century, and is not meant to supersede the rich and detailed work of previous historians of the union and its predecessors, but merely to bring its story down to the present day. Those interested in delving deeper into the union's past will perhaps benefit from the guide to further reading at the end of the book. The records of the National Union of Seamen and the National Union of Railwaymen are on deposit at the Modern Records Centre, University of Warwick Library.

This work would not have been possible without the contribution of members of the union. I would like to place on record my thanks to those RMT members who took the trouble to share their thoughts about the union's recent past, including Alan Pottage, John McDonald, Mick Atherton, Keith Erskine, Peter Trend, Gerry Hitchen, John Milligan, Bob Rayner, Mick Thompson and the late John Cogger. Particular thanks are due to Geoff Revell, who has guided the project through with a mixture of sage advice, gentle prodding and singular good humour. Needless to say where they are not directly quoted the opinions expressed here are my own, and any errors and omissions are mine. I would also like to record my thanks to Carla Mitchell for her wise counsel and unstinting support, and to Samuel Berlin for forever lifting my spirits.

# Introduction

THIS BOOK TELLS THE STORY of the last 27 years of the RMT, one of the most traumatic periods in the history of the British labour movement. For 17 years from the election of Margaret Thatcher in 1979 there was an all out assault on Britain's trade unions, through legislation and the courts, combined with the wholesale privatisation of a huge portion of British industry. In the name of 'free enterprise' and 'efficiency', the last quarter of a century has witnessed the decimation of entire swathes of traditional industries as whole communities throughout Britain were laid waste by the Thatcher government's pursuit of economic dogma. During this period the trade union movement put up a brave if often rearguard resistance to Thatcherite attacks on workers' rights and state-owned industries. The labour movement was divided against itself with a mostly older generation of conservative union leaders often reluctant to take action in the face of new anti-strike legislation engaged in internecine battle with a more radical rank and file. The Labour Party, faced with successive Conservative electoral successes and the setting-up of the breakaway Social Democratic Party, was also dogged by internal dissension. Thatcher's confrontation with the unions came to a climax with the miners' strike in the spring of 1984–85 when the National Union of Miners took on the government over plans to close up to 20 pits. Refusing to recognise Tory legislation mandating a vote before strike action, the miners' union found itself liable to prosecution through the courts. Though individual unions did all they could to help, the Labour Party leadership proved to be unable or unwilling to come to the miners' aid.

The resulting defeat of the strike was a huge setback to the trade union movement. With the subsequent privatisation of the coal industry, it looked as though the Tories' aim of destroying the power of organised labour was on the verge of total victory. In the process Britain's industrial landscape was changed forever. Traditional industries in which Britain had led the world were allowed to wither. Thatcher's government held a virtual fire-sale of nationalised industries: everything from coal and steel down to the provision of hospital and school meals were sold off to the private sector. In transport important national industries such as shipbuilding and railway manufacture were shrunk to a fraction of their former size or allowed to disappear altogether. Municipal and rural bus services were privatised, as were airlines and ferry services. Only the national rail network eluded Thatcher's grasp and when she left office in 1990 it fell to the ill-fated government of John Major to go for one last great privatisation. The sell-off of the publicly owned railways between 1994 and 1996 has by common consent been one of the greatest disasters in the history of British public administration. British Rail, a by no means perfect but truly national transport network, was shattered in a hundred pieces in pursuit of a completely spurious notion of competition with results that are still with us.

Meanwhile the Labour Party in opposition moved from resistance to Thatcherism to an acceptance of most of its main tenets. In pursuit of electoral credibility the party abandoned many of its original aims. Whether or not it is seen as a recognition of economic reality or a cruel betrayal of a hundred years of struggle, the abandonment of a commitment to the idea of common ownership, symbolised by the ditching of Clause 4 of the Labour Party's constitution before the election victory of May 1997, was a turning point in labour history. A new Labour government came to power on a great groundswell of opposition to 17 years of Tory rule. But it did so in part by distancing itself from the ideals of the very trade union movement that created it.

But despite the apparent success of Thatcherism in the late 1980s and early 1990s the trade unions did *not* wither away. Far from caving in to 'the triumph of the market', activists in the RMT and other unions never gave up the fight to maintain workers' rights. Instead they held out against the onslaughts of Thatcherism, adapted to changed circumstances and worked together, across a broad front of campaigns and organisations, to reinvigorate trade unionism. The creation of the RMT in the spring of 1990 through the merger between the National Union of Seamen (NUS) and the National Union of Railwaymen (NUR), unions which could trace their histories back over a century to the Victorian age of sail and steam, marked a new beginning. Throughout the past 27 years the men and women of the RMT have played a central role in resisting the assaults against the labour movement and have rebuilt their union as a strong campaigning organisation. The renaissance of organised labour was the work of tens of thousands of ordinary members of the RMT. This is their story.

It is also the story of earlier generations of trade unionists whose battles for workers' rights created the modern trade union movement. The predecessors of today's members of the RMT played a crucial role in the genesis of the industrial and political wings of the labour movement. The early history of the railway and maritime unions is one of bitter struggles against oppressive and intransigent employers who abhorred the very idea of collective rights for workers and worked through parliament and the law courts to strangle the new unions at birth. In the face of these powerful forces, the trade unions of the late Victorian period looked beyond the established political parties to the creation of a new voice in parliament that would truly champion the cause of the working class. It was the direct antecedent of today's RMT, the Amalgamated Society of Railway Servants (ASRS), which sponsored the 1898 meeting that led to the creation of the Labour Representation Committee, the forerunner of the Labour Party. In 1899 Richard Bell, Assistant General Secretary of the ASRS, became with Keir Hardie, one of the first Labour MPs to be elected to parliament. The infamous 1901 Law Lord's judgment in the case of the strike on the Taff Vale railway, which made trade unions liable for damages during official picketing, convinced many of the need for an independent voice in parliament. In 1903 the ASRS began levying members 1s per year to support the Labour Representation Committee. This was challenged by one of the ASRS' own branch secretaries, Walter Osborne of Walthamstow, who with the backing of the *Daily Express* newspaper took the union to court. The 1909 Osborne judgment in the House of Lords, which went against the ASRS and prohibited the unions from making payments to their sponsored MPs, further encouraged trade unionists in their belief in the necessity of parliamentary representation to counter the anti-trade union prejudices of the law lords and the courts. The genesis of the Labour Party was thus the result of recognition by trade unionists that the right of workers to legally organise themselves could only be secured by parliamentary representation by and for the labour movement, independent of the two main political parties.

The trade unionists of a century ago also began to make a broader connection between workers' rights and the struggle for a more just and equitable society. They increasingly looked to relatively new and radical ideas, such as industrial syndicalism, common ownership and socialism, to achieve this. The NUR in particular was born amidst the tumult of the great unrest of the early twentieth century, when careful nurturing of a parliamentary voice for labour was combined with vigorous pursuit of industrial goals. The NUR rulebook of 1912 uniquely committed the union to the aim of working for 'the supercession of the capitalistic system by a socialistic order of society', words still enshrined in the union's rulebook today. The doggedness of their efforts, in the face of overwhelming economic and political odds, provides parallels for the modern history of trade unionism. This book is an attempt to place the last 27 years in this wider context of the history of the struggle for social justice in modern Britain.

# 1
# *Sail and Steam*

THE ROOTS OF TODAY'S RMT go back over a century to the Victorian period when the industrial landscape was marked by traditional heavy industries in which Britain led the world. In coalmining, steel production, railway construction and shipbuilding Britain was the leading industrial power. Working conditions on the railways and aboard ships of the merchant navy were harsh in the extreme. Employers were effectively self-policing autocrats who imposed wages and working conditions. The railways were run with military efficiency that combined a martinet like approach to industrial relations with a sometimes paternalistic attitude to employee welfare. Fines for minor infractions and instant dismissals were combined with a rigid grade hierarchy. Railway companies provided an entire way of life for their employees, with their own housing, schools and even churches. Shipboard life was equally disciplinarian, though far less secure than that of the railwaymen. Ships' officers exercised quasi-judicial authority over men at sea. Food, pay and accommodation aboard ships were grim. Ship's fo'c'sles were rife with damp and disease. Corrupt and violent ships' agents, known as 'crimps' preyed on seafarers in ports, arranging signing on and payment for ship owners, after forcing seamen into debt. Ship owners, eager for profit, routinely overloaded vessels turning them into notorious 'coffin ships' which easily capsized in heavy weather.

The National Union of Seamen, the maritime element of today's RMT, traces its origins back to public campaigns against these dreadful conditions. The campaign by the great reformer Samuel Plimsoll, MP for Derby, 'the sailors' friend', who succeeded in passing the Merchant Shipping Act 1876, which attacked overloading, led to a greater awareness of safety at sea and spurred seafarers themselves to organise. Earlier moves to unionise sailors had failed. In 1851 a short lived 'Penny Union' was created as a national union but fell apart after a lock out one year later. Thereafter ad hoc attempts to form so-called port unions, which functioned as friendly societies for sailors, gave way to more permanent attempts to create a national union. The National Union of Seamen had its origins in the Amalgamated Sailor's and Fireman's Union of Great Britain and Ireland, founded in the port of Sunderland in 1887. The seafarers were led in the early years by the mercurial figure of James Havelock Wilson, a Sunderland able seaman who went from being a firebrand leader of the lower decks during his youth to becoming an arch reactionary who stoutly took the side of the bosses in old age. Elected as Liberal MP for Middlesbrough in 1892, Wilson became an opponent of attempts at forming a separate party of labour in the early 1900s.

## New Unionism: Militancy and Amalgamation

Wilson's union came into being at the dawn of the era of so-called 'new unionism', when groups of previously non-unionised workers in shipping and other industries began to organise not on the basis of the older craft-based associations but on industry-wide lines. The new unions were highly politicised and strongly influenced by the then extremely radical idea of common ownership of major industries, to be pursued by either legislative nationalisation or through the direct workers control achieved through a general strike. Manifested in the success of the great London dock strike of 1888, in which tens of thousands of casual and unskilled dockers came together to strike for better wages and conditions, New Unionism made itself felt across Britain. In the aftermath of the great dock strike Wilson's union earned a reputation for militancy, reaching a high point in terms of numbers in the early 1890s with some 65,000 members in some 60 branches. The shipping bosses created the Shipping Federation in direct response to the new union. The Shipping Federation organised strike breaking, transporting blackleg seamen in ocean-going tugs to break up disputes which succeeded in breaking up Wilson's union. Its successor organisation, the National Sailors' and Firemen's Union (NSFU) took years to rebuild an organisational presence in the shipping industry. The high point of shipboard militancy came in the great year of unrest, 1911, when Britain's seamen staged a series of strikes, led by the NSFU in conjunction with Tom Mann and Ben Tillet's International Transport Workers Federation, bringing Britain's ports to a standstill. The seamen's action provided a powerful spur to other groups of workers, including railwaymen. At Cardiff, where the seamen's strike was a scene of violence and arrests, employees of the Great Western Railway, the railway company servicing the port, came out in sympathy. At Liverpool a general strike was declared as Winston Churchill sent a cruiser and armed troops against the seamen and dockers, as thousands of railwaymen took to the streets in sympathy. This solidarity formed part of a new wave of activism amongst transport workers, including members of the ASRS who staged the first national railway strike in August 1911.

As a result of the 1911 port strikes the seamen's union succeeded in gaining official recognition from the Shipping Federation, but in the aftermath of the 'great unrest' Wilson led his union into an open alliance with the employers. Wilson became a fervent nationalist during the First World War, stamping out any hint of pacifism in the seamen's ranks and going so far as to prohibit his members from allowing Labour leaders to travel to the continent at the height of the war to discuss peace proposals with fellow German and other European socialist leaders. Wartime control of shipping labour brought about the creation of the National Maritime Board, which oversaw national collective bargaining. After the war Wilson became a zealous anti-socialist, working hand in glove with the Shipping Federation against more radical breakaway unions such as the Amalgamated Maritime Workers Union. Wilson's union, renamed the National Union of Seamen in 1926, refused to back the General Strike that year. Wilson provided support for the renegade Spencer union, set up by employers to sap the strength of the Miners Federation, and providing assistance for court action aimed at challenging the legality of the strike. The Trades Union Congress (TUC) duly suspended the seamen's union from membership for a period of four years. Though reunited with the TUC in 1928 it was to be many years before the NUS ridded itself of the reputation of being a 'bosses union' among fellow trade unionists.

The railway element of today's RMT followed a separate but related path of development. The National Union of Railwaymen was also a product of the great wave of unrest of the early twentieth century, though with a more central if no less controversial role in the wider labour movement in the years before and after the Great War. Founded in 1913 the NUR was a result of the amalgamation of three older unions: the Amalgamated Society of Railway Servants, founded in 1871, the General Railway Workers Union, founded in 1880, and the United Pointsmen's and Signalmen's Society, founded in 1889. The oldest of the three, the ASRS, was founded at the Winchester Arms, Southwark, at a meeting presided over by the MP for Lambeth, Thomas Hughes, a lawyer and social reformer who was to find fame as the author of *Tom Brown's School Days*. Grade chauvinism was a persistent barrier to union organisation in these early days, allowing employers to divide workers on the basis of wage differentials between grades. The NUR was one of the first attempts at founding an 'all industry' union in Britain. 'All industry' unions derived their inspiration from syndicalist ideas which sought to create powerful unions comprising all groups of workers within a major sector of industry. But the aim of creating one industry-wide organisation eluded it. After unsuccessful overtures to get the Associated Society of Locomotive Engineers and Firemen (ASLEF), founded in 1880 as a craft based union for footplate workers, to merge with the NUR, relations between the two were to be characterised by alternating periods of competition and cooperation. Later a separate white collar union, the Railway Clerks Association, was set up. The aim of creating powerful alliances of organised labour was pursued further in 1914 when the NUR sought to join with the miners and transport workers to form the famous Triple Alliance to provide a united front in negotiations with employers, but these plans were postponed by the outbreak of war.

## The Great War, the General Strike and the Depression of the 1930s

The sacrifices of the Great War of 1914–18, in which some 18,957 railwaymen and over 19,000 merchant seamen were killed on active service, paved the way for a great outpouring of demands by trade unionists for improvements to conditions when the guns fell silent. Wartime conditions had brought state direction of industry and the active participation of the unions in aspects of wartime administration. The state direction of the railways seemed to presage the possibility of some form of common ownership. The slaughter of the trenches, combined with the worldwide political and social upheavals that followed, including the 1917 Bolshevik revolution, set the scene for a post-war confrontation between capital and labour. Under government control during the war, the railways made special 'war bonus' payments to railway workers with regard to the long hours needed in wartime conditions. At the end of the war the railway employers were anxious to see a return to controlling their private fiefdoms, rolling back wages and conditions to pre-war levels. The government of Lloyd George engineered a showdown with the railway workers, going so far as to make preparations to use the army to break any strikes that might result.

The nine-day national rail strike of September 1919 was marked by an overwhelming display of solidarity by the trade unions. Support for the strike was near total. ASLEF and the NUR, led by General Secretary J.H. 'Jimmy' Thomas, worked together for the first time. Though members of the peerage jumped at the chance of fulfilling childhood fantasies by driving trains as blacklegs, few railway workers followed their example. Instead huge demonstrations were held up and down the country with concerts, church services and football matches, some between army units and union branches, being held to raise funds and keep up spirits. With the prospect of the strikes spreading to other industries, an active intervention of a delegation of other unions pressured Lloyd George's government to settle.

The NUR emerged from the 1919 strike as one of the most powerful groups of industrial workers. The strike also brought to a head proposals to rationalise the organisation of the railways. Lloyd George's government, which had previously publicly contemplated nationalisation, opted instead for the creation of four national railway companies, 'the big four', out of the 120 pre-war rail companies in the Railways Act, 1921. Amalgamation of the railway companies gave the NUR a greater possibility to bargain across the transport sector. But paradoxically the strike served to weaken the potential for creating broader coalitions with the other trade unions. NUR General Secretary

Thomas did not call on the pre-war Triple Alliance to assist in the 1919 strike. When the Miners Federation went on strike in 1921 the NUR initially promised to support them through the Triple Alliance but Thomas, having just won significant concessions for his members and fearing the political consequences of widening the miners' action, withdrew support for a strike in sympathy. Thomas' action led to the ignominious collapse of the Triple Alliance on 15 April 1921, 'Black Friday'. Though Thomas was elevated to high office in the minority led first Labour government of 1924, MacDonald's government cold-shouldered the trade union movement. The labour movement from this period became arrayed into two interdependent and sometimes mutually hostile wings: the industrial and the political.

The difficulties of organising across these divisions were to be demonstrated to the full during the May 1926 General Strike. What began as a sympathy strike in support of the Miners Federation soon turned into the largest industrial action in British history. The role of Jimmy Thomas, who engineered a return to work on 12 May without consulting the miners' leaders, is one of the most controversial in labour history and is widely seen as a great betrayal of the miners' cause. His disloyalty to the miners should be understood in the context of the general trend in the attitudes of the leadership of the unions in the late 1920s and early 1930s. By the time of the first Labour government of 1924, in which Thomas had served as colonial secretary and organised the Empire Exhibition at Wembley, the leaders of the larger unions were establishment figures, their militant days behind them, and with little predilection for confrontational class politics. Thomas had become a *bon viveur*, hob-nobbing with the establishment and sending his sons to public school. The NUR had by this stage a significant voice in parliament, in the form of four directly sponsored MPs. In the wake of the failure of the General Strike most of the membership, faced with the prospect of mass unemployment, were inclined to follow a path of conciliation. This did not prevent the emergence of a more radical rank and file movement within the union. The Minority Movement, influenced by the recently formed Communist Party, sought to challenge the complacency of leadership of the NUR under Thomas. It attracted a significant following but remained what its name implied, a minority movement, though one of its leading lights, Jim Figgis, went on to become General Secretary after the Second World War. From the early

1930s the left within the NUR coalesced around the Railway Vigilance Movement. The sectarianism of the Communist Party's adherence to the 'class against class' line then emanating from the Soviet Union during the late 1920s and early 1930s, which led it to denounce the leaders of the TUC and the Labour Party as 'social fascists', alienated many and limited the left's influence.

The deepening world depression of the 1930s left transport workers vulnerable to the cold wind of unemployment. With profits down the big four railway companies sought and achieved big cuts in wages and conditions in 1931. The second Labour government, in which Thomas was given the critical task of dealing with unemployment, was unable to stop the growing lines of the dole queues. Thomas supported MacDonald's proposal for a cut in weekly allowances to the unemployed. The ultimate ignominy of the Thomas period in the NUR's history came in 1931 when he followed Ramsay MacDonald into office as a member of a conservative dominated coalition National government. The NUR regarded this as a gross betrayal of the labour movement, expelling Thomas from the office of General Secretary and from union membership, withholding his pension. In the ensuing general election the National government was re-elected and Labour, which had also expelled MacDonald, Thomas and the other renegades, lost a swathe of seats. For the first time in 30 years there were no NUR sponsored MPs. The NUR, along with most of the other unions, was on the defensive for the remainder of the 1930s. Attempts to get the railway companies to restore the cuts imposed in 1931 were only partially successful by 1937. During the recovery of the mid 1930s the railway companies were able to pay 4 per cent dividends to shareholders but unable to raise wages above 50s per week. This was at a time when the Quaker philanthropist Joseph Rowntree found that a family of four could not adequately survive on less than 53s per week. But the union was unable to get the railway companies to budge on the most basic issues. Growing unemployment plus the looming spectre of fascism and war dampened expectations of what could be achieved through industrial activism.

### The Second World War and Nationalisation

The contribution of the trade union movement to the defence of Britain and the ultimate defeat of fascism during the Second World War needs to be restated, because it helps to explain the tremendous outpouring of support for a Labour victory in the 1945 general election but also the great expectation of social change that accompanied it. The enormous sacrifice of the British people, a sacrifice in which some 300,000 merchant seamen and railwaymen served in the merchant navy and the armed forces, brought about an enormous transformation in social attitudes.* The coordination of all aspects of national life in pursuit of the common goal of victory through the state direction of industry demonstrated the possibility for coordination and cooperation in peacetime. The suffering of the British people during the war, combined with the experience of state intervention in the provision of basic welfare services, led many to believe that the post-war world could not and would not mean the return to the poverty and unemployment of the hungry 1930s.

In the realm of transport one of the ultimate hopes of trade unionists was the nationalisation of the railways. As early as 1894 the ASRS had committed itself to the ultimate aim of the public ownership of the railways, and members of the NUR looked with high hopes to the incoming Labour government. The Transport Act 1947 which nationalised the railways under the British Transport Commission began a 50-year experiment in public ownership. In the event the experience of nationalisation for railway workers proved to fall short of the hopes which had animated the original advocates of public ownership. For the NUR nationalisation was always envisaged not merely as bringing control of the nation's transport under state direction but also as a means of extending the participation of the workforce in the direct management of industry. For many in the NUR public ownership without worker participation meant no more than exchanging one set of employers for another: instead of dealing with boards of directors the union now negotiated with ministers and senior civil servants who were no more sympathetic than their old bosses. Indeed most of the management of the nationalised railways were of necessity hangovers from the days of the private railway companies. Attempts by General Secretary Jim Figgis to press the Labour government on the issue of worker participation were snubbed. In an era of full employment wages

---

* The Merchant Marine Memorial at Tower Hill, London, records that some 24,000 merchant seamen died at sea in the Second World War.

and conditions of railway workers lagged behind those of other groups of workers.

Much needed modernisation was slow in coming, with the Labour government concerned to direct resources to other areas of expenditure, especially the newly created National Health Service. Generous compensation payments to former shareholders also hampered investment. After the election of the Conservatives in 1951 the Tories sought to roll back the tide of nationalisation, and the 1953 Transport Act encouraged privately run road haulage companies, hastening a shift of freight traffic from rail to road. In 1955 the government gave the go-ahead for what seemed to be a programme of radical modernisation; new stations would be built, marshalling yards mechanised, steam locomotives would be replaced by diesel and electric traction. But the rise of car ownership was sapping the receipts of British Railways and by the early 1960s the Conservatives decided to pull the plug on their hitherto ambitious plans. The NUR, led by the dapper right wing Labour loyalist Sidney Greene, proved to be unable to prevent what was to come.

## Beeching and After: Labour in and out of Power

The infamous axe wielded to the national network of rail services by Dr Richard Beeching, appointed as Chairman of the British Transport Commission by the Conservatives in 1961 after a career spent as a chemist for ICI, gravely undermined the central place of the railways in the national life. Beeching's proposals cut something like over 30 per cent of the existing network, destroying whole provincial branch networks and leaving entire parts of the country with a skeletal service. The steady increase in car ownership, coupled with government programmes of road building, encouraged by the powerful road haulage and road construction companies, gradually ate away at passenger numbers and freight traffic. The links between the road lobby and leading politicians of the Conservative Party, such as Ernest Marples, Beeching's boss, who founded one of the construction companies responsible for building the M1 motorway, in part helps to explain the sorry state of the railways in the post Beeching era. But successive governments of both parties starved British Rail of investment. The Ministry of Transport in the 1960s and 1970s was always a Cinderella service in terms of government expenditure, a relatively easy area to make savings in tough times. The ministry was led by a revolving door of politicians with sometimes little interest in their brief. The attitude of the political classes to Britain's railways in this period was summed up in the words of Tony Crosland, environment secretary under Harold Wilson's 1974 government, who was said to have remarked: 'transport is a great bore'.

Successive governments made promises to improve rail services which they failed to keep once in office. Though the administration of Harold Wilson came to power in 1964 on a promise to halt the Beeching cuts, once in office it continued the closure programme. The Transport Act 1968, piloted through by Barbara Castle, did something to reverse the decline of the railways. The establishment of British Rail Engineering Ltd by the 1968 Act paved the way for further modernisation of the railway workshops. But the overall response of later governments was poor. The Heath administration proposed further cuts and the Labour manifesto of October 1974 promised that if elected it would aim 'to move as much traffic as possible from road to rail and to water, and to develop public transport to make us much less dependent on the car'. Once in office Labour, seeking to hold back inflation after the oil crisis of 1974, gradually retreated from this aim. Harold Wilson's government at first gave British Rail a substantial investment of £2.1 million and passed the 1974 Transport Act, which through the Public Service Obligation gave grants to keep up investment. This resulted in a new wave of improvements, including the introduction of fast diesel High Speed Trains and InterCity services. But in the second half of the 1970s transport policy shifted towards the roads. Labour announced cuts in subsidies in autumn 1975 and this led to 50 per cent rises in rail fares that year. The aloof Tony Crosland was hostile to the railways and the railway unions, failing to even meet the newly elected NUR General Secretary Sidney Weighell. In 1976 Crosland issued a consultation document that advocated further cuts to services. Crosland adopted the view that railways were for the middle classes, and favoured investment in road transport, including buses, coaches and private cars.

The NUR responded to Labour's proposed cuts with a campaign which exposed the potentially deep divisions between the trade unions and the government. A public slanging match developed between

Crosland and Weighell, with the minister's suggestion that the union's claims were 'a load of old codswallop' being responded to by the typically acerbic comment by Weighell that Crosland was a 'bloody liar'. So bad did relations get that the union contemplated telling the NUR sponsored MPs to withdraw support from the government. Sidney Weighell justified the suggestion on the grounds that:

> 'There was no good reason why my union should go pouring money into the Labour Party and giving faithful support to the Government, if they refused to listen to us.'

The irony of Weighell's comments, coming from an ardently loyal and rigorously right wing trade union leader, deserves to be remembered in light of the subsequent history of the union. Though Weighell was accused of breaching parliamentary privilege, and was hauled before the House of Commons, neither he nor his union were threatened with expulsion from the Labour Party.

As a result of the piecemeal modernisation accompanied by a stop-start approach to funding, by the 1970s the working life of members of the NUR and the other rail unions was massively transformed. The previous era had seen the replacement of steam by diesel and electric locomotives. In the 1970s new technology, in the form of the new InterCity 125s, automated push-button power signal boxes, ticket machines, computers, and new freight handling and track maintenance equipment, altered the way of life on the rails. Traditional grades such as shunters, linemen, firedroppers and steamraisers disappeared. New responsibilities were added to traditional jobs as guardsmen became responsible for additional duties such as ticket collection, porters for station supervision and workshop staffs gained skills such as electrical engineering.

Established working practices were modernised, often through negotiated settlement with the NUR and the other unions in return for improvements to pay and other conditions. But for many workers the brave new world of the 1970s, which had seen much manual work abolished, lacked the sense of camaraderie of the previous age of steam. Far fewer people worked on the railways. The transition to diesel and electricity, combined with the impact of the Beeching cuts and subsequent modernisation had led to a big decline in the workforce, and subsequently union membership, by the end of the

1970s. By 1980 the total workforce of British Rail, including hotels and catering, engineering, goods yards, permanent way staff, signalling and locomotive drivers and guards stood at 170,000, down from 390,000 in the mid 1950s. Despite this, union density remained high, and affiliation to the Labour Party was strong.

> Looking back now they were the glory days. We had a closed shop. My branch, Euston branch, at that time had 2,300 members and only two did not pay the political levy. We had one of the best records of any trade union in the country for paying the political levy. Yes, we had tremendous support.
>
> John Cogger

Those who remained in the years after Beeching found themselves facing new pressures and challenges. A gradual but significant decline in accidents and fatalities to railway workers (as well as passengers) was matched by increased instances of illness due to stress and physical assaults on staff. New anti-social hours, the decline of gang work and a consequent loss of a sense of shared identity were among the less tangible effects of these changes on the railways.

### The Decline of the Red Ensign: Globalisation and the British Merchant Marine

Changes in working practices were no less traumatic for the seafarers. The 1960s and 1970s witnessed a dramatic reversal of fortune for Britain's merchant shipping fleet. Traditional forms of employment for seafarers disappeared as a result of changes in technology and new patterns of world trade. The break up of the British Empire led to the loss of traditional colonial trade links as newly liberated ex colonies looked elsewhere for major trading partners. Commercial jet travel replaced ocean-going passenger liners; container ships, roll-on roll-off ferries, specialist bulk carriers and super tankers took the place of the general purpose multi-deck ships, tramps and cargo liners.

The British merchant fleet, built up at the height of the age of empire, can be seen to have been amongst the first victims of the globalisation of world trade since the 1970s. Two key developments of this period

The reason the UK fleet was so large was that the bulk of it was in cross trades between Australasia and the developing world, India, the Philippines and the Pacific rim. That was a regular trade. They used to call it the 'crusader trade'. British merchant ships were charted and used to run regularly between the States and Australasia. You could get on one of those ships and not get off for two years. The decline started with the conversion of the Empire into the Commonwealth and the absolute need for developing countries to try to control and carry their own trade. That didn't last very long. Flags of convenience were created which was a way of avoiding taxation and higher crew wages. The major factor in the decline of the UK merchant fleet was the loss of the cross trades. That was the start of the decline.

Bob Rayner

stand out. The first was containerisation, using uniform 8-foot square by 20-foot long metal units, which standardised cargo handling and fully automated the loading and unloading of ships. First developed by the United States Lines in the early 1960s, containerisation steadily spread to the world's trade routes. In 1969 the *Encounter Bay*, built for the British shipping conglomerate Overseas Containers Ltd, began what was to be the world's first container service plying an international trade route between Australia and Europe. The spread of containerisation in the late 1960s marked a new era in the globalisation of world trade with vast implications for the working lives of mariners. Whereas a standard ocean-going cargo vessel of the pre-container period might require as many as 30 to 40 deck hands the new container ships could be crewed by fewer than ten men.

The other great change to sweep over the industry was the development of 'flags of convenience' whereby ship owners transferred registration of their vessels from their countries of origin to 'open registry' countries. Begun in the 1920s by US shipping interests as a means of evading legislation to protect the health and safety of US seafarers, the use of out flagging to countries such as Panama and Liberia took off in a dramatic way in the 1950s and 1960s. The US merchant fleet virtually disappeared though British ship owners, buoyed by the continuing expansion of world trade during the 1960s, added ships to the national register. Though the number of vessels declined, the size of the British

merchant fleet, measured in terms of gross tonnage capacity, continued
to be one of the world's largest.

There was a decline in the 1960s and early '70s. Despite the losses of
the Second World War there was still a lot of old tonnage around, and
there had been a building programme in the '40s. I was on several of
those ships. There was a replacement programme to build tankers and
dry cargo vessels but then there were rapid changes in the industry, with
the economics of the oil industry meaning that you needed larger and
larger ships. Those large fridge ships which were built after the war were
becoming suddenly virtually obsolete. They needed huge crews. The
ship I was first on in '63 had four quartermasters, eight ABs, four boys,
a senior quartermaster, a lamp trimmer, two bosun's mates, a bosun,
four fridge greasers, four donkey greasers, a donkey man, a storekeeper
and six main greasers, half a dozen engineers, four apprentices, a fourth
mate, third mate, second mate, chief officer and master. She carried
a maximum of 12 passengers. You had a maximum of 80-odd crew. A
lot of derricks, and the old fashioned type of very small hatches in the
middle of the ship, and big fridge lockers in the side. Depending on the
season, we sometimes used to bring holds full of lamb back or holds
full of apples, particularly from Tasmania. The advent of container ships,
new methods of cargo carrying and handling and the age of these ships
did away with all that.

Bob Rayner

The attitude of the NUS leadership to these changes was ambiguous.
Unwilling to move on questions of modernisation, the union
leadership was also following Havelock Wilson's traditional policy
of working closely with the ship owners' organisations, at first the
Shipping Federation, then the General Council of British Shipping.
The National Maritime Board oversaw working agreements. Despite
improvements in the 1950s, wages and working conditions at sea
remained relatively poor.

The seamen's strike of May to July 1966 in part reflected the
frustrations of a younger generation of seafarers who were left behind
by the rising tide of prosperity of their landlocked brethren and who
also felt let down by the lack of militancy of the NUS leadership.
Remembered today for Harold Wilson's denunciation of the supposedly

There was a history of quite appalling treatment. My father was down below throughout the last war. He served throughout the hostilities. He joined in 1938 and went right straight through the war and briefly left the industry after hostilities and was back at sea until he had an accident in the '50s. He can recall that people worked one day a week throughout the war without pay at all. When I came to sea the big issue, as it is with the RMT today, was the working week. To try and negotiate reasonable pay and conditions we ended up briefly with an increase in the working week. The advent in the late 1960s and early '70s of consolidated pay rates meant that you ended up in some trades on an unlimited working week. That was unpopular. Because of the low base rates we always relied on overtime. The only area where we made any inroads was the amount of time one stayed on a ship. When I first went to sea you always signed two year articles, so if the vessel was on the liner trades down to Australasia you could generally guarantee you came back to the UK in four to five months and you would then get the opportunity to pay off. But then because of the transition to boxed freight, the container trade, it meant that the cycles were more accurate because the vessels were like massive conveyor belts going around the world as they are now. Most articles became six months because there was very little need to have anything longer than that. There weren't any advances made without struggle by seafarers.

Bob Rayner

communist influence of 'a tightly knit group of politically motivated men' and for precipitating a sterling crisis, the strike was led by a younger rank and file reform movement which had begun to emerge and pressure for better conditions, including the future Deputy Prime Minister John Prescott. The reform movement partially succeeded in taking control of the union with the election of leading reformer Jim Slater in 1974, an affable veteran of the Atlantic convoys. Though the long-term decline of the merchant fleet was not halted, the demand for fewer larger specialist vessels meant that the industry faced shortages of skilled labour. The short-lived *Sealife* initiative, sponsored by the National Maritime Board, sought to investigate and improve conditions to make the industry 'more attractive to the UK seafarer' in order to enhance and retain skilled labour. Like the NUR, the leadership of the seamen's union in this period sought to work with the voluntary limits of Labour's social contract, though the policy of wage restraint angered many in the NUS and in 1976 the union came close to calling another national strike. Thereafter for the remainder of Labour's term in office the union leadership tried to work within the voluntary 10 per cent limit on pay claims advanced under the social contract despite vociferous opposition from significant sections of the rank and file. The NUS did much in this period to get over the reputation for complacency hanging over it from Havelock Wilson's day. Under Slater's leadership the NUS in conjunction with Greenpeace, successfully stopped the dumping of nuclear waste at sea, opposed the Falklands War of 1982, and later gave support to the miners. Jim Slater's time as General Secretary was marked by attempts to democratise union structures, opening up the union to ordinary members and giving greater representation to the rank and file, always a difficult task amongst as far flung a body as seafarers.

The manpower shortages of the 1970s aboard ships encouraged the ship owners to increase the number of non-domiciled seamen serving in the UK merchant fleet. The employment of seamen from British colonies, at far worse standards of pay and conditions, had long been a feature of the merchant navy. For centuries Asian sailors or Lascars had served on British ships plying the Indian Ocean. In the era of steam large numbers of Chinese, Yemeni and Somali seamen crewed as stokers on British merchant ships, working in atrocious conditions and at vastly inferior rates of pay. The early British seamen's unions operated strict colour bars, and saw all non-white labour as a threat to wages and conditions. In the 1970s the hiring of 'non-dom' seamen expanded greatly. By 1976 more than 17,000 seamen from countries such as Bangladesh, Hong Kong, Pakistan and Sierra Leone were working on UK registered ships. From 1974 the NUS agreed to an annual £15 levy to be paid to the union for each 'non-dom' sailor employed by the owners. Denounced by many members of the NUS as immoral and racist the levy effectively perpetuated the two tier nature of international shipping with seafarers from third world countries suffering far lower standards of wages, conditions of service, and health and safety than their first world counterparts. The institutionalisation of these double standards came in 1976 when, under pressure from the ship owners, the Wilson administration exempted merchant shipping from the

1976 Race Relations Act outlawing discrimination in employment and other areas.

The internationalisation of manpower in British shipping presaged even more dramatic developments. With the rise of state subsidised Japanese and more importantly Korean shipbuilding by the late 1970s there developed a massive overcapacity in worldwide shipping. Overcapacity combined with the post oil crisis recession in world trade hit British shipping particularly hard. The response of British shipping interests was to cut costs by selling, scrapping or re-registering their fleets under flags of convenience. The gross tonnage capacity of the UK registered fleet contracted by 30 per cent between 1974 and 1979. During this period many of the famous shipping lines, which had sailed the world in Britain's industrial heyday, disappeared. By the end of the 1970s the gross tonnage of the UK fleet was a mere 4 per cent of the world total. The seamen's union sought to counter these trends by working through the International Transport Federation and the United Nations Conference on Trade and Development to enforce international standards through minimum, so-called 'blue flag', standards but also through concerted campaigns, taken in conjunction with the shipbuilding unions and other interested organisations, to get governments to do something to stem the dramatic decline of the British merchant fleet and the conditions of its seafarers. The introduction of a tonnage tax by James Callaghan briefly led to an increase in UK registered vessels, though this initiative was short lived. Though the situation seemed grim in the later 1970s, after the Tory election victory of 1979 the hope of any positive action to support British shipping disappeared.

## Beer but no Sandwiches: the NUR before 1979

The situation on the railways was more positive in the years before Thatcher's election. During this period the NUR also worked with others to improve transport; coming together with other organisations, including transport campaigns, amenity societies and the newer environmental pressure groups to lobby for a public voice for public transport. Transport 2000, an initiative of Sidney Weighell, was created in 1972 to campaign for an integrated national transport strategy. At the same time, the parliamentary voice of transport workers was strengthened by the enlargement of the number of NUR sponsored MPs from 4 to 11 with a full-time political liaison officer to coordinate their work, making the NUR the best represented trade union in the House of Commons.

To a certain extent these efforts were successful. Public campaigns succeeded in persuading the Labour government under Jim Callaghan, once Tony Crosland had been replaced by the more rail friendly Bill Rogers, not to implement previously proposed cuts. Support for British Rail (BR) through the PSO system enabled BR to reopen some of the stations Beeching had shut. The reorganisation of BR into stand-alone businesses, including InterCity and Network South East, succeeded in attracting new passengers. By the dawn of the Thatcher era BR had gone some way towards reversing the tide of decline.

A deteriorating economic and industrial climate prevented it from doing so. Despite modernisation the wages and conditions of railway workers lagged behind their counterparts in other comparable jobs. British railway workers were amongst the worst paid in Europe by the mid 1970s. In the aftermath of the defeat of Edward Heath's loathed Industrial Relations Act of 1971 a policy of voluntary wages restraint was tried, under the Social Contract, whereby the Labour government set voluntary wages targets in consultation with the management and unions of the nationalised industries. Inflation, which soared to 25 per cent after the oil crisis, undermined this as groups of workers such as miners and power workers put in above inflation wage demands. The result was to ratchet up the inflationary cycle as other unions, including the NUR, sought to put in comparable claims. A crisis over rail pay developed in 1975 as the traditional negotiating mechanism, the Railway Staffs National Tribunal, broke down over the NUR's rejection of BR's final offer of 21 per cent. A national rail strike was only averted by the direct intervention of Prime Minister Harold Wilson. Despite differences over policy, the historical and political importance of the NUR meant that the rail union's governing body could maintain close relations with the Labour cabinet when engaged in bargaining over pay.

The future of Labour's Social Contract and the NUR's support for it looked shaky after the pay crisis. General Secretary Sidney Weighell found himself increasingly isolated both from other trade union leaders and the national executive of his own union. Condemning the pursuit of

> I was fortunate enough to be on the executive when we went down for midnight beer and sandwiches and I can now disprove the story. There were no sandwiches and all we had was a cup of warm beer out of one of those seven pint kitchen tins but at least we were in the cabinet room, all 24 members of the NUR executive talking to Harold Wilson, Michael Foot, people of that ilk.
>
> John Cogger

inflation-busting pay claims through a return to free collective bargaining as 'the philosophy of the pig trough', Weighell succeeded in persuading the NUR to adhere to the Social Contract. In a series of closely fought votes by the union's national executive and at annual conferences in 1977 and 1978 support for the Social Contract was re-affirmed but at the price of exposing the growing divide between the union's executive, who saw themselves as representing the voice of the rank and file, and Weighell, who became the trade union movement's most vociferous advocate of Labour's policy of wage restraint. Weighell also faced opposition from other trade unions. The train drivers' union ASLEF rigorously sought to return to free collective bargaining and relations with the NUR were dogged by traditional sectionalist infighting. The NUS also faced off against the Callaghan government's wage restraint policy. The Social Contract fell apart as other members of the TUC went back to free collective bargaining. When Callaghan's government announced a 5 per cent pay target in August 1978 and the TUC general council rejected it the stage was set for a series of damaging public sector strikes that winter. What went down in history as the 'Winter of Discontent' was in fact limited to groups of poorly paid local council

> Up to that point, although it was never a bed of roses, there was always work. Up to that point our people could always make a living. Our disputes were mainly over pay increases in order to get a decent rate of pay, in the '60s, '70s and early '80s. We were fighting for conditions which were appalling in some places, still had gas lights in some of the marshalling yards and signal boxes. But we had some of the best machineries for protecting people. We would love to have them back now.
>
> John Cogger

and National Health Service employees, but the strikes demonstrated the vulnerability of Labour's economic policy and irreparably damaged Labour's chances in the general election of 1979. Perhaps the trade unions would not have rushed back into free collective bargaining with such speed had they realised what was waiting in the wings. In the event the defeat of the Labour government by the Conservatives in the general election of May 1979 marked the beginning of one of the bleakest periods in trade union history, though few at the time could have predicted the severity of what was to come.

# 2
# Into the Abyss

THERE WAS LITTLE INKLING OF the offensive on trade unionism when the new Tory government came to power in May 1979. Their plans for transport were spelt out in a seemingly innocuous document, *On the Right Track*, written by Tory transport spokesman Norman Fowler in 1978, which merely promised that any incoming Tory government would seek to introduce a measure of competition of transport services 'where appropriate, as in the provision of road haulage and some long distance bus services'. The Tory election manifesto was similarly anodyne. No mention was made of privatising Britain's public transport network; there was some indication of intentions to de-regulate long-distance bus networks and private sector 'partnerships' with publicly owned businesses, though with government retaining the majority interest in these concerns. Historians are divided on the extent to which the incoming Thatcher government had a worked-out plan of wholesale privatisation. Though the idea of privatisation of Britain's railways had been mooted by the Conservative Research Department as early as 1968, and through the 1970s privatisation became the mantra of the more extreme fringes of the Conservative Party and the then shadowy think tanks such as the Adam Smith Institute and the Centre for Policy Studies, nothing in the Tory Party's election literature could give a hint of what was to come. Privatisation was in its early days a haphazard, opportunistic affair. Many 'wets' within the first Thatcher government were old style corporatists and the more hardline free marketeers had to accommodate them. Thatcher's personal dislike of the railways was a matter of historical record: she was alleged to have rarely travelled by train and was a firm believer in what she called 'the great car economy'.

Behind the scenes there were signs that the Tories were planning an assault on the more important trade unions. According to his memoirs, Nicholas Ridley, one of the architects of Tory privatisation plans, had asked fellow Tory Keith Joseph to prepare a report on privatisation which included a secret annexe on how to defeat the unions in the event of a strike by the miners. These plans included the use of private haulage firms and the organisation of a mobile police force. These were the origins of what came to be known as 'Ridley's list': unions, including the NUR, which were to be targeted by an incoming Tory government with a raft of new legislation designed to roll back union power.

Once elected the Tories undertook the piecemeal hiving-off of state owned transport assets. First to go was the National Freight Corporation, privatised by Act of Parliament in June 1980. Created under Barbara Castle's 1968 Transport Act, the National Freight Corporation consisted of two subsidiaries, Freightliners Ltd and National Carriers Ltd. £100 million of taxpayer's money was poured into the business by the Tories to fatten up the industry prior to the sell off. Sold for £53.5 million to a group of UK banks, the majority of the equity shares in the renamed National Freight Consortium went to the Company's managers and 13,000 staff. Eventually, pay and conditions of service were to be negotiated on a local basis and the freight industry lost more than 10,000 jobs by 1984.

The same act provided that long-distance express bus services, hitherto dominated by the publicly owned National Bus Company (NBC), should be opened up to private competition. The deregulation of the long-distance bus routes was significant for several reasons. The act paved the way for the rapid decline of rural bus services as the NBC's subsidiaries responded to competition by withdrawing cross-subsidies of rural services. It also gave rise to a new wave of private bus companies such as Stagecoach, owned by the right wing entrepreneur Brian Souter, which rapidly sought to undercut the NBC's long-distance routes. The private companies had a significant impact on BR's revenues as passengers moved from relatively expensive train travel to the new coach services. The new coach companies went on to play a prominent role in rail privatisation, buying up many of the franchises to run rail services.

The next to go were the 29 British Transport Hotels (BTH), which encompassed hotels and rail catering, including the famous golfing hotels at Gleneagles and St Andrews, under the Transport Act, 1981. Traditionally poorly paid and difficult to organise, workers in the hotels and catering branches of the railways had benefited from three decades of sustained attempts by the NUR to better their wages and conditions. Under the 1981 Transport Act, BTH was split up and the more profitable hotels sold on to the highest bidder. At first the NUR was able to reach an agreement with the new owners to maintain wages and conditions, but as the other hotels were sold the union later found itself having to negotiate with up to 13 separate companies, with often unscrupulous managements who discouraged union membership, a foretaste of things to come.

The election of Thatcher ushered in one of the most acute recessions in modern British history. Under the direction of Chancellor of the Exchequer Geoffrey Howe the government stood by as unemployment soared to a level not witnessed since the depression of the 1930s. The Howe slump had a direct impact on the demand for transport. By 1979 BR was carrying more passengers than in any year since before the Beeching era. During the subsequent slump fewer people travelled by rail and industry had less need of rail services to move goods and materials. Demand for locomotive stock and other forms of railway engineering work were affected by a worldwide downturn in demand for rolling stock. The new Tory government added to the increasing misery of BR's finances by almost immediately cutting the amount of borrowing that BR could call upon each year. The so-called External Funding Limit (EFL), the amount of money BR was given by central government, was cut by some £15 million in June 1979.

The Tories also began to introduce an ad hoc series of new laws designed to limit trade union rights to organise and take industrial action, carried out by the vociferously right wing employment minister Norman Tebbitt. The 1980 Employment Act outlawed so-called secondary action by restricting picketing to places of employment except under strict legal criteria, as well as limiting the closed shop and trade union rights to statutory recognition. In 1982 another Employment

Act virtually outlawed sympathy strikes, tightened further the rights of unions to closed shop membership and, crucially, made unions liable to injunctions and civil suits by employers. Mrs Thatcher had often spoken of her desire to return to Victorian values. For trade unionists this meant turning the clock back on virtually a century of progress to the days of Taff Vale and the Osborne judgment. More punitive legislation was enacted in the years to come.

The fortunes of the NUR during the early Thatcher period were closely bound up with the controversial personality of the General Secretary Sidney Weighell. Born in Northallerton, Yorkshire, of a railway family, Weighell went to work for London and North Eastern Railway as a teenager and worked as NUR organiser for 21 years before becoming General Secretary in 1975, a career broken only by two years as a professional footballer for Sunderland FC. His private life was marked by tragedy: just before Christmas 1956 his wife and four-month-old daughter were killed in a car accident. Descriptions of Weighell vary from 'clearheaded, forceful, courageous' to 'a combative, spiky character' to 'remote, humourless and dictatorial'. A leading figure on the right of the labour movement Weighell was closely involved in the party infighting which followed Thatcher's election victory. Along with Bill Sirs of the Iron and Steel Trades Confederation (ISTC), Roy Grantham of the Association of Professional, Executive, Clerical and Computer Staff, and Terry Duffy of the Amalgamated Union of Engineering Workers, Sidney Weighell was a member of what came to be known as the 'St Ermin's Hotel group' (known after the Westminster hotel which had long been a location for political intrigues) which formed the bastion of the Labour right within the TUC and were derisorily known to their opponents as the 'St Ermin's Tendency'. Weighell also sought to revive the old 'Triple Alliance' of the 1920s in conjunction with Bill Sirs of the ISTC and Joe Gormley of the National Union of Miners (NUM).

Weighell saw himself as a great moderniser, who would drag his union kicking and screaming into the twenty-first century, through productivity deals with British Rail, that would inevitably involve job losses but which it was hoped would secure better conditions for those who kept their jobs. Weighell's unwillingness to brook opposition from within his own union led him to label any alternatives to his policies as dangerous subversion. His term in office was marked by attempts

> Weighell would talk about the saving of the industry rather than the saving of jobs as such. Of course if there is no industry there are no jobs. Advancing the pay and conditions of members and jobs was less important than 'protecting the industry'. His clash that he had was with his executive, not just with the left on the executive, because he managed to unite left and right. He managed to unite them by stifling any debate that might make fighting back against the bosses succeed, because he would not rock the boat. That was never on his agenda and he went to enormous efforts to stymie the democratic structures of the union.
>
> Geoff Revell

to impose his will on the NUR and increasingly acrimonious infighting within the union. Weighell sought to stamp his mark on the union by undertaking a vast building project, the construction of a new union headquarters. The old Unity House on the south side of Euston Road, completed in 1910, was a much loved Edwardian pile, richly decorated inside and famed in trade union annals as the scene of great events such as the General Strike of 1926. Weighell turned his back on this rich heritage, citing the need to build a dynamic and modern image for the union. Unity House was demolished in 1980 and the new building, a modern if anonymous glass office block, known as 'the black box', was opened further along Euston Road in 1983. During the crucial first years of Thatcher's onslaught against the unions Weighell became almost obsessed with his pet projects. Another project was the purchase of a manor house and 44 acres of grounds at Frant Place, Kent, as an education centre. Opened in 1977 Frant Place was a useful addition to the union's training facilities, though Weighell's choice of chief education officer was Ben Stoneham who was later a founder member of the breakaway SDP.

It was during Weighell's time as General Secretary that the NUR's sponsorship of MPs was substantially reorganised. In 1975, acting on a proposal by Derby No. 3 branch, the union sought to increase representation in parliament by changing the method by which the sponsored MPs were selected to allow for the adoption of already elected MPs. By this means the number of MPs sponsored by the union rose to eleven and came to include some of a new generation of

MPs who would become leading figures in the parliamentary Labour Party, including Robin Cook, Frank Dobson, Donald Dewar, Tam Dalyell and Donald Anderson. An important innovation was the appointment of a full-time political liaison officer, Keith Hill, whose role was to coordinate the activities of NUR sponsored MPs, using the resources of the union's research department to help draft reports and parliamentary questions. NUR sponsored MPs met monthly to coordinate their activities, with each member specialising in different aspects of transport policy. What came to be known as the 'NUR group' was increasingly recognised as one of the most effective trade union sponsored groups of MPs in the House of Commons. It is important to note, in light of what has subsequently transpired, that activities of the NUR group were aimed at representing the best interests of the union in parliament, in collectively coordinating parliamentary activity to influence transport policy. Sponsorship of the RMT group did not merely imply influence, it was its main purpose.

Weighell's period in office was also marked by a series of internal reforms that were designed, in his eyes, to streamline and update working procedures of the union. In 1981 he commissioned Warwick University Department of Industrial Relations to embark on a report that recommended the reorganisation of the NUR's Executive Committee. The system of geographical representation of different grades on the Executive Committee was overhauled to give a bigger voice to hitherto underrepresented grades including buses, road and freight, workshops and London Underground. Paradoxically these reforms undermined Weighell's position. When he began to lose support during the period 1980–81, the representatives of these grades on the union's executive were a direct point of contact with those members who were suffering most from the government's policies.

The £15 million cut in the EFL forced British Rail to try to implement a new round of productivity deals. The NUR responded by stating that it would only accept any new arrangements in return for significant improvements to working conditions, including a reduction in the working week, improved basic rates of pay and lengthened annual holidays. These demands were put to the British Rail Board at a meeting at the Great Western Hotel, Paddington in August 1979 and formed the basis for a detailed plan for negotiations, the so-called *Railwaymen's Charter*, drawn up by the NUR in September. The *Railwaymen's*

*Charter* proposed a £60 per week basic rate of pay, with extra for staffs and skilled grades, a 35-hour working week phased in over five years, four weeks annual leave plus an adoption of the continental system of rostering whereby workers did four or five shifts over seven days, with Sunday to be treated as any other day. In return for agreeing to this more flexible system of allocating work the NUR demanded compensation for anti-social hours and promises to defend and improve the existing rail network. Members of the union could be forgiven for thinking that the *Railwaymen's Charter* was a reasonable set of demands given the sacrifices they had already made for the sake of productivity in the late 1970s. They were soon to be disabused of any illusions that the new government was willing to deal honestly with the industry.

The BR board under Sir Peter Parker responded to the *Railwaymen's Charter* by proposing a programme of productivity improvements and job cuts, spelt out in a document entitled *The Challenge of the Eighties*. This envisaged radical reorganisation of the manning of trains, introducing a new grade of 'trainman' to replace and amalgamate the grades of conductors and guards, the progressive running down of the older marshalling yards and the collection and delivery of parcels, with up to 30,000 job losses in return for improvements to basic rates of pay, weekly hours and annual pay. Meanwhile the NUR, ASLEF and TSSA (Transport Salaried Staffs' Association) cooperated in a joint approach in the 1980 pay round. After the NUR EC's rejection of BR's initial offer of 13 per cent plus 4 per cent for productivity improvements, BR agreed to pay the full 20 per cent increase demanded by the union plus a 39-hour week and improved annual leave. In return the unions agreed to accept the reorganisation of the marshalling yards and the freight and parcels service.

As the recession deepened the financial position of BR deteriorated. In November 1980 Parker called a 'crisis summit' of the BR board and the rail unions at Watford. Parker announced that BR needed to borrow some £972 million just to avoid cuts in services. Any hope of getting the government to raise the EFL rested on reaching an agreement on modernisation. The result of the Watford summit was an agreement, 'the Balance Sheet of Change', which committed BR and the unions to enter into detailed negotiations on issues such as one-man operation on motive power traction units, the introduction of unmanned or 'open'

> We were fighting against job cuts from 1979 right the way through to the miners strike. The battle within the union itself was about trying to advance our wages to be sure, but also against 'rationalising' the workforce, Driver Only Operation, this programme of British Rail, 'the roadshow' we called it, where British Rail management were going around with these graphs and charts, with a kettle boiling and steam going into a tube and drips of water coming out with targets. They were saying 'things are going to change'.
>
> Geoff Revell

stations, and flexible rostering. Weighell secured the agreement of the union's executive to pursue the proposals laid out in the 'Balance Sheet of Change' and to join with BR and the other rail unions to approach Tory transport minister Norman Fowler together. A meeting with Fowler was held in late January 1981. He seemed to indicate that the government would be willing to agree to more investment and modernisation, especially the electrification of the network and improvements to conditions, in return for concessions by the unions on flexibility and rationalisation of services. But even had the minister been willing to deal fairly with the unions, subsequent events were to knock away any plans for a policy of compromise.

In September 1980 David Howell replaced Norman Fowler. He initially appeared to adopt a conciliatory approach by raising the EFL to £950 million. Howell followed Fowler in linking any further investment in modernisation with acceptance of changes in manning and operations. Howell hinted that the government was on the verge of giving the go-ahead to a ten year programme of electrification. But in early 1981, as BR revenue dropped further, negotiations between the unions and BR over pay broke down. In the 1981 pay round BR's offer of 7 per cent was improved by the Railway Staffs National Tribunal, chaired by Lord McCarthy, to 8 per cent plus a further 3 per cent for improved productivity. This was initially rejected by the BR board which would only agree to the extra 3 per cent in return for widespread de-manning and flexible rostering. Negotiations collapsed and the NUR and ASLEF threatened to hold an all-out national strike to start on 31 August 1981. Intervention by ACAS (Advisory, Conciliation and Arbitration Service) led to talks between the BR board and the rail unions, with Sidney Weighell acting as joint spokesman for the unions. After three-day marathon talks it appeared an agreement was in reach. Detailed discussions centred on manning and the role of guards. Ironically, given subsequent events, the issue of flexible rostering was not extensively discussed. The leaders of the three rail unions agreed to a timetable for negotiating productivity agreements, including flexible rostering, in return for the McCarthy award. This timetable signed up the unions and BR to an arrangement to settle by 31 October 1981. During the autumn of 1981 flexible rostering went from being a relatively technical negotiating point to a minor *cause célèbre* as the joint union approach broke down. The NUR agreed to implement flexible rostering whereby the working day would vary around the eight hour day. ASLEF by contrast opposed any changes to the principle of the eight hour day. The BR board refused to implement the McCarthy award until ASLEF agreed to flexible rostering.

Relations between the NUR and ASLEF became increasingly strained after ASLEF leader Ray Buckton announced that the union had decided to call a two-day national strike for 13 and 14 January 1982 against the flexible rostering agreement. A separate strike by ASLEF members taking action against an agreement which the NUR had already signed up to put the two unions directly at odds. Further acrimony was caused on the second day of the strike when the BR board agreed to pay NUR members the McCarthy award of 3 per cent extra. The two-day strike led to infighting between and within ASLEF and the NUR. NUR members were extremely reluctant to cross ASLEF picket lines. While ASLEF members and some in the wider trade union movement saw the failure of the NUR to go out in sympathy as a betrayal of trade union solidarity, some inside the NUR felt that Sidney Weighell was wrong to sign up to flexible rostering in the first place and he faced angry meetings of London based NUR guards. As Weighell's memoirs show, he suspected opposition to flexible rostering within the NUR was being fomented by what he termed the hard left. The ASLEF–NUR dispute has been interpreted as reflecting a widening rift between left and right within the trade union movement. But what should be remembered is that many on the left within the NUR, while accepting the merits of ASLEF's case, did not think that flexible rostering was an important issue of political principle nor the best point on which to challenge the Tories' transport policies.

In the aftermath of the first flexible rostering strikes in January 1982 the Tory attitude to the rail unions hardened and their real intentions became clear. Transport Secretary Howell refused to implement the McCarthy award in full until a settlement was reached on flexible rostering. At the same time the attitude of the BR board toughened and in the 1982 pay round it offered a derisory 5 per cent but only on condition that the ACAS agreement of 1981 be fully complied with. The threatened closure of the Shildon works in County Durham by BREL, with the loss of 2,450 jobs in a town of 11,000 inhabitants plus losses of a further 3,000 jobs at Swindon and Horwich worsened the atmosphere between BR and the NUR. The union successfully used the threat of industrial action to win a temporary reprieve for the workshops. Strike action was threatened for the end of June 1982 unless the workshop job cuts were rescinded and BR's pay offer was substantially improved. The BR board announced in early June that Shildon would not be closed nor would it make cuts at Swindon and Horwich. But the board refused to budge over pay. Meanwhile, a fortnight of lightning strikes by ASLEF members from 5 to 18 June over flexible rostering added to the mood of industrial militancy. Within the NUR there was a division over strike tactics. Instead of the selective action favoured by Weighell the executive voted in favour of an indefinite all-out strike for 27–28 June, in what was to be the first national walk out since 1955. The second day of the strike coincided with the NUR annual conference, due to be held at Plymouth, when the 77 delegates temporarily exercised executive powers as the union's parliament. At Plymouth debate centred on how long the strike should go on for. Though eager not to be seen as less than wholeheartedly supportive of the strike, Weighell let it be known that he thought continuing industrial action was 'counter-productive'. After several hours debate the Plymouth annual conference voted to suspend the strike after 24 hours.

There is no doubt that at the 1982 Annual General Meeting, Sidney Weighell was in the ascendancy. He was a formidable figure and certainly in control at the AGM, where the meeting certainly reflected his position as far as industrial matters were concerned. It is ironic, therefore, that the Plymouth AGM sowed the seeds of his downfall.

John Milligan

The flexible rostering strikes and the Plymouth conference were marked by an increasingly bitter confrontation between Weighell and the union executive and sections of the union. Weighell was convinced that he was being undermined by a hard left conspiracy, made up of members of the Militant Tendency, the Socialist Workers Party (SWP) and others within the union. Since June 1981 a NUR 'Broad Left' group, with its own publication *Left Lines*, was created and campaigned for a more radical approach to dealing with the Thatcher government. During the 1982 strikes some members of the Broad Left sought to support striking ASLEF members and among London based guards' meetings were held to organise unofficial action. Weighell later claimed that during this period the balance on the executive moved in favour of his opponents, with according to him some 12 of the 26 seats on the Executive Committee (EC) being held by members of what he termed the extreme left. But there is another way of looking at these developments. The constitution of the NUR always gave a significant voice to the union's rank and file, through direct election of union officials and the union's annual conference. According to Weighell the democratic structure of the union made it unmanageable: 'I sometimes think we have democracy run mad.' Branch meetings and the union's annual delegate conferences were traditionally highly politicised forums. The left had always had a strong voice in the NUR; some but by no means all of Weighell's critics in the union were aligned to Militant or the SWP. His personality was more than enough to guarantee that he would attract opposition. Weighell's very public championing of Dennis Healey against Tony Benn during the 1981 campaign for the deputy leadership was bound to seep into union politics.

Weighell became increasingly convinced that the left within the union were out to get him. By the time of the flexible rostering strikes some branches were openly challenging his position and papers began to be circulated at district councils and national grades meetings calling for a change of leadership and direction. Under Rule 10 of the NUR rulebook the circulation of pamphlets and other material was prohibited unless authorised by the EC or the General Secretary. Weighell used this rule to clamp down on his opponents' literature and began to collect a dossier of evidence of what he claimed was subversive activity within the union. Complaints of infiltration were received from over 50 branches. The Plymouth district council passed a resolution against the circulation of such material and asked the executive to punish those responsible. Five union members, including one member of the executive, Ian Williams, were identified as 'subversives' and their names included in Weighell's dossier presented to the executive. Weighell's characterisation of Williams as subversive is ironic. Williams later went on to be instrumental in overturning Militant domination of Liverpool City Council. A sub-committee of the executive was set up to investigate these claims, packed according to Weighell with hard left supporters. It nevertheless came out against the circulation of unofficial material and found Williams and two others in breach of Rule 10, asking that they desist from further activities in this regard. The executive voted 17 to 7 to reject the sub-committee's findings and Weighell responded by making a direct appeal to the membership. A widely reported speech by Weighell to NUR branch secretaries at Chester, attacking Tony Benn and his followers as a 'rabble' who should leave or be expelled from the Labour Party, attracted a letter from 15 executive members disassociating themselves from his views. In the run up to the Plymouth conference Weighell became increasingly paranoid. He pointed to a photograph of several members of the EC handing a £100 cheque to ASLEF leaders, published in the *Morning Star*, as further evidence of subversion. He came to believe his post was being opened, took to standing away from station platforms and asked for police protection at union meetings.

> Unlike Sidney Greene before him, who was as right wing in labour movement terms as you could get but who had total respect for the democratic structures of the union, Weighell wanted to close down those structures so that we wouldn't fight, couldn't fight. His attack on the left developed into attacking anybody who didn't agree with him. He would lump everybody as a 'subversive Trotskyite'. The democratic structures of the union were there but the union's apparatus can be used in the wrong hands to close those structures down.
>
> Geoff Revell

At Plymouth in June 1982 a three hour debate was held on 'subversive activity' within the union. Delegates from the floor attacked the executive for not taking more forceful action against the circulation of unofficial material by Militant supporters and others. One delegate suggested that Williams and other executive members who had written or spoken out in defiance of union policies should be expelled from the union. In the end the conference voted to overturn the executive's decision not to punish those found guilty of violating Rule 10 and imposed a £10 fine and warning. From that point on the battle lines between Weighell and members of the executive were drawn.

These tensions fed into wider conflicts within the Labour Party in the run up to the October 1982 party conference at Blackpool. Despite his defeat in the deputy leadership elections Tony Benn's supporters within the party were still pressing for changes to the party's constitution. The composition of the party's National Executive Committee (NEC) became a crucial battleground in the contest between the left and right of the party. Traditionally elections to the trade unions section were governed by an informal and often highly complicated set of rules that worked against political factionalism. Membership of the trade union section of the NEC was designed to reflect union membership strength as well as the seniority of the union within the labour movement. Some unions, including the NUR, entered into informal agreements to use their block vote to support NEC candidates from other unions. Under the revived Triple Alliance the NUR, ISTC and the NUM had supported each other's candidates to the NEC elections by trading votes. Intra party conflicts between the left and right undermined these relationships. The right wing leaders of the St Ermin's Hotel group began to target the left on the NEC. Elections to the 18 trade union positions on the NEC became increasingly politicised as the St Ermin's group manoeuvred to alter the rules governing elections in order to remove the left. The NUM's candidate to the NEC Eric Clarke had previously been elected by the use of the NUR's block vote, and the NUR's candidate, Russell Tuck, had likewise been elected with the miners' support. The previous July the NUR's Plymouth AGM had passed a resolution moved by Bristol No. 3 branch that the NUR again support all the previous nominees to the NEC. In a highly ambiguous speech to the Plymouth meeting Weighell appeared to endorse this, telling the delegates, 'In the world in which we deal for seats on the party executive and seats on the TUC general council, there are unions that trade votes. That is the world you and I live in.' He interpreted the resolution as meaning 'they are saying we have got a nice, sensible, balanced party executive which will lead us into the next General Election in some sort of unified form. If you want unity you will support this resolution.' But come the Labour Party conference Weighell cast the NUR's block vote for a representative of the EETPU, the electricians' union led by leading right wing trade unionist Frank Chapple.

Weighell later justified his subsequent behaviour by saying that he found it impossible to cooperate with the newly elected NUM President Arthur Scargill, who succeeded Joe Gormley in April 1982. His actions between the time of the Plymouth AGM and the party conference suggest he was playing an elaborate game designed to deny the NUM a seat on the NEC. In early September he took the unusual move of formally writing to the NUM asking if it would trade its vote for Russell Tuck in return for the NUR's support for Eric Clarke: 'in the spirit of the Triple Alliance, the NUR will be supporting NUM nominees for the TUC General Council and General Purposes Committee and for the Labour Party National Executive Committee and Conference Arrangements Committee. I will be pleased to hear you are doing the same in the case of the NUR nominees for these positions.' Putting such deals down on paper was thought to be highly irregular and rather than a written response the NUM General Secretary Lawrence Daly verbally agreed that the NUM would vote for Tuck. Weighell made no mention of any change in voting intentions at the August TUC conference, when representatives of the various unions canvassed support for the NEC elections.

When the Labour Conference convened at Blackpool on 27 September voting for the NEC was one of the first major items of business. Weighell made no contact with the NUM delegation, seated only a few yards away in the conference hall, nor did he inform his fellow NUR delegates of his intentions. Only once the vote was taken was it found that Eric Clarke's tally was a million votes short and that he had lost his place on the NEC. Weighell was asked whether he had voted for the NUM's man and, according to NUM delegates, confirmed that he had. A re-count was held and it was discovered that the scrutineers had failed to count 600,000 NUPE votes for Clarke. As a result Arthur Scargill and Moss Evans of the Transport and General Workers' Union (TGWU) were eventually allowed into the scrutineers' room and, after looking at the tabulations of the vote, soon realised that Weighell had gone back on his agreement.

On the second day the results were announced and it had gone against the wishes of the union's parliament. Eric Clarke of the Miners had not been voted on to the NEC. We arrived in the hall and there were all sorts of rumours flying around about the validity of the vote. Down at the end of the aisle I saw Arthur Scargill crouched over talking with Sidney Weighell. The conversation was about how the NUR votes had been cast. Weighell told him that 'my vote was in accordance with my union's position'. A delegate came back and said we were on the news. Weighell became animated. We started to ask what was going on. The miners had asked for a recount. The Steel union leader Roy Grantham let it be known that if moves were made to reopen the ballot boxes that he would seek a court injunction. Two members of the conference organising committee, Bob Kettle, a highly respected Labour Party activist and ex member of the NUR executive, and Eric Bristow of the NUM, were allowed to check the ballot papers. Bob Kettle realised by looking at the tally that the NUR votes had not been cast for Eric Clarke. I was sitting two seats away from the union's President Tommy Ham who said, 'conference will end soon. We are being filmed by the media. I want you to come orderly to back of the stage where we are borrowing Michael Foot's office and where we will have a discussion about what's going on.' And I said 'It's us, isn't it? It's f\*\*king us, isn't it?' He wouldn't reply. In Michael Foot's office Weighell's line was astounding. He told the meeting: 'yes it was true' and that although our parliament had said that we had a slate that included Eric Clarke it was a 'wheel and deal' situation and that as he had no assurance from the miners that they would support our nominee to the NEC that he decided to cast our vote for someone else. When asked by John Milligan why he didn't tap Scargill on the shoulder and ask him how the NUM would vote he said he had written to the miners and had not received a reply. A decision was then taken to write a report to the executive but that in the meantime that no one at the meeting would speak to the media. We were coming out of Michael Foot's room and leaving the auditorium. Running past us was every journalist under the sun, cameras, lights flashing. So we turned around and followed them back to find that Weighell was standing there and holding a press conference. The most awful thing that he said was 'I have explained the situation to my delegation and they are satisfied', which was just a blatant lie.

Geoff Revell

When the news of Weighell's chicanery came out the NUR and NUM delegations reacted with bemusement and fury. Weighell quickly left the Blackpool conference, and according to his memoirs, contemplated his future on the ride back down the M1. He remained convinced that he had acted correctly, and later claimed that he felt that the lack of written response had freed him from any obligations to the NUM. He had 'interpreted' the Bristol No. 3 resolution as he thought in the best interests of the union. An unofficial meeting of the executive in London decided to take moves to suspend him. Rather than face the ignominy of formal suspension, which would have immediately removed him from office, Weighell tendered his resignation to the executive on 6 October 1982. Under union rules this meant that he remained in post for a further three months.

Weighell and his supporters hoped that he could muster enough support for his position to remain in office longer, and that at the union's Special General Meeting due to be held in Birmingham in mid October, a resolution would be put forward that he be asked to reconsider his resignation. The SGM was also to decide on the important matter of whether or not to accept the award of the McCarthy pay tribunal. At Birmingham a motion was put forward by York branch asking him to withdraw his resignation but the meeting voted by 41 votes to 36 to accept his resignation offer. Weighell, who waited in a nearby hotel to hear the result of the vote, was livid. He nevertheless came back to the hall to give a dramatic speech in favour of accepting the McCarthy pay award. It was his last public speech as General Secretary and it was sufficiently persuasive to influence the meeting to vote decisively in favour of the pay award. Weighell's breach with the executive was complete. There was to be no false exchange of polite words or thank

---

The Weighell episode was traumatic because no one had sacked the General Secretary before. It showed that corrupting votes would not be tolerated. It was hoped the vote was a new direction, a fresh start. That the union would be opened up to its membership. That everybody could have a say what we were going to do. That there would be debates and people would be encouraged to take part in their union's affairs, that the union would be opened up.

Geoff Revell

you cards. When Weighell's pet project, the new Unity House, was finally opened in May 1983 he was pointedly not invited to attend. The new Unity House lasted only some seven years before it too was demolished in 1990, in a final ignominious end to the Weighell era. Though Weighell's tenure in office had achieved many things, including the strengthening of the NUR's parliamentary voice, the establishment of Frant Place and the reorganisation of the Executive Committee, the constant infighting which his leadership engendered did not leave the union in the best place to combat the challenges which lay ahead.

# 3
# The Miners' Strike

THE DOWNFALL OF SIDNEY WEIGHELL coincided with the beginning of
the last great confrontation between the Thatcher government
and the trade union movement. In the aftermath of the victorious
Falklands War Thatcher held a general election in early June 1983. The
Tories romped home to a second general election win and the more
ardent Thatcherites were emboldened to push ahead with their plans to
make Britain into a supposedly free market paradise. A new, even more
draconian union-busting law was introduced. The 1984 Trade Union
Act made pre-strike ballots compulsory four weeks before withdrawal
of labour, forced elections every five years for union executives and
compelled unions to hold ballots on political funds. At the same time the
Tories pursued a programme of wholesale privatisation, beginning with
energy, telecommunications and steel, and extending to other major
industries including transport. By the time of the second Tory victory
the government's agenda of progressive erosion of the public sector, the
hiving-off of nationalised industries and all out assault on trade unionism
was already in full swing. The showdown with the unions came with
the twelve-month miners' strike which began in March 1984.

For transport workers these developments were marked by a series
of bitter local struggles that led to a further erosion of their wages
and conditions, and inevitable job losses. At sea and on land the early
1980s were a time of setbacks, lost strikes and limited victories. Tens
of thousands of workers across a range of transport industries lost

their jobs: engineers at the BR workshops, deckhands on cruise ships, cargo handlers in ports, railway engineering shopmen, shunters in marshalling yards and numerous others. Both the NUS and the NUR sought to campaign and take action against the attacks on the industry but were limited in what could be achieved by the new Tory anti-union legislation. During the miners' strike both unions gave solid support for the miners' struggle and many members defied Tory laws to render aid, but in the aftermath of the miners' defeat there was great demoralisation. The spread of Tory privatisation policies to transport, a haphazard and ad hoc process to begin with, went much further. The beginnings of a new era of globalisation of world trade, marked by the increasing economic liberalisation, anti-union legislation and the rapid mobility of capital had begun. Trade unionists struggled to find new ways of organising and combating these trends.

## The NUS before the Miners' Strike

For the seamen the early 1980s was a period of bitter ironies. They had seen their industry dwindle as ship owners and the slick men of the Baltic Exchange made a killing by flagging out. During and after the 1982 Falklands War, in which many NUS members took part as members of the Royal Fleet Auxiliary, the government basked in the reflective glow of a display of British maritime power while thousands of merchant seamen were cast on the scrap heap. The ultra nationalist rhetoric masked the utter indifference of the Tories to pleas to protect British shipping and shipbuilding. During the year 1982, dubbed 'Maritime England Year' by the British Tourist Board, some ten thousand mariners lost their jobs.

The NUS fought doggedly but unsuccessfully to defend jobs during the Thatcher period. The leadership of the union encouraged a new period of greater activism as seamen took strike action against threats to their jobs. Jim Slater, elected General Secretary in 1974 and Sam McCluskie elected Assistant General Secretary in 1977 and General Secretary in 1986, both sought to extend the union's activities, encouraging the formation of shipboard branches and a more engaged deep-sea membership. A successful month-long worldwide strike was staged in January 1981 which forced the employers organisation, the General Council of Merchant Shipping, to go to arbitration about overtime.

In the aftermath of the strike, Canadian Pacific, which had settled separately with the NUS, was expelled from the General Council. As a result shipping employers began to disengage from the traditional bargaining and employment mechanisms, the National Maritime Board and the Merchant Navy Establishment, as a means of negotiating with the NUS. The old ways of working were breaking down.

There were other, smaller victories. In 1980 the NUS successfully persuaded Trafalgar House to keep the *Cunard Countess* in UK registration and in 1981 the union convinced P&O not to sell four refrigerated ships and charter them back under a flag of convenience. But these successes were followed by even greater difficulties for the industry. The Falklands War was something like the last demonstration of the importance of a national merchant navy, and in its aftermath, de-manning and out-flagging of the fleet was relentless. The UK fleet shrank by two-thirds between 1975 and 1985 by re-registration and sales for scrap. Cross-Channel ferries and cruise ships now became one of the most important areas of the NUS' work and on board these ships NUS members took action in defence of jobs. A series of strikes took place on the ferries and cruise ships between 1982 and 1985. An important symbolic victory was won in 1982 after a six week sit-in by the crew of the Sealink ferry *Senlac* at Newhaven which temporarily reprieved the cross-Channel service to Dieppe and Le Havre. Successful strikes were staged against Townsend Thoresen during the busy summer season in 1983. On board the cruise ships the biggest issue was the replacement of stewards and other service and catering crews by poorly paid 'concessionaire' crews, recruited from third world countries. There was also a strike by seamen against P&O but in 1986 600 NUS members aboard the *QE II* accepted redundancy packages from Cunard and were replaced by a concessionaire crew. Between 1979 and 1987 more than 13,000 ratings were lost from the register of merchant seamen, 21,000 were de-registered with the specialist employment offices for seamen shut in all but seven ports.

The deregulation of worldwide shipping, the spread of flags of convenience and the consequent decline of wages and conditions of seamen advanced like a great wave in the 1980s. Safety standards, hitherto upheld through the national registration system, were now left to international minimum safety norms. Members of the Organisation for Economic Cooperation and Development adopted these in 1976 in response to pressure from the NUS and other maritime unions represented in the International Transport Workers Federation, but standards were often poorly enforced on open registry ships. The Thatcher government did all it could in these forums to push through liberalisation and free trade. Beyond publicly campaigning and taking individual action against selective targets there was little the union could do to stem the haemorrhage of jobs.

## The NUR after Weighell

Transport workers on land faced different challenges from the same neo-liberal onslaughts of the Thatcher government. The fall of Sidney Weighell came at a critical moment for the NUR. Weighell was succeeded in early 1983 by Jimmy Knapp. Knapp joined the railways as a signalboy aged 15 and took up his first union post aged 18. After many years as a regional organiser he became a headquarters officer in 1981. Though he initially failed the written exam for the post of Assistant General Secretary (there were allegations that the exam paper questions had been loaded against him) he was elected General Secretary in March 1983. Knapp's election was seen as a victory for Weighell's opponents and Knapp was cast as a creature of the far left within the union. Weighell was particularly caustic about Knapp's relationship with his old enemies, attributing Knapp's election to the machinations of the extreme left. Still being quoted in the press an almost hysterical Weighell called him 'wet behind the ears, a stooge of the Communists and Trotskyite left'. To which Weighell's opponents countered: 'better wet behind the ears than mucky hands'. One of Knapp's defeated opponents for the post, Assistant General Secretary Andy Dodds, in an effort to boost an election campaign doomed before it began, publicly accused Knapp of being a 'tool of the militants'. But the union ranks were by now fed up with these nonsensical outbursts and wanted change. Knapp's real opponent was Charlie Turnock who as Assistant General Secretary was seen as the natural successor. However, Turnock though better known than Knapp, was considered by the majority, rightly or wrongly, as having been too close to Weighell. Knapp won by a landslide majority. Like his NUS counterparts Jim Slater and Sam McCluskie, Knapp was part of the broad left within the labour movement, but his later action in support of Neil Kinnock's attempts to purge the Labour Party of Militant supporters (largely left to Turnock to propagate within the union) and his arguments within his executive to stop them 'going to the wire' on Tory anti-trade union legislation hardly suggests he was a creature of the union's far left after his election. His 17 years as General Secretary, down to his death aged 60 in 2001 have been variously seen as a period of consolidation and rebuilding or as a time of drift. Loathed in the right wing press as a trade union 'dinosaur' and mocked for his thick Ayrshire brogue, Knapp was personally liked within the labour movement. But some within the NUR saw the 'big man' as a weak and vacillating leader whose period in office is referred to as 'the grey years'.

## The Serpell Report

Knapp's period in office came amidst a fresh wave of new Tory legislation on privatisation and trade union rights. The recession of 1982 led to a decline of rail traffic, and with a rising deficit, BR was subjected to the scrutiny of a four-man government commission on railway finances, headed by Sir David Serpell, a former senior civil servant. The commission also included Alfred Goldstein, linked to the Thatcherite guru Professor Alan Walters, who reputedly helped secure his appointment, as well as the neo-conservative Alfred Sherman, James Butler, senior partner of Peat Marwick Mitchell, a consultant on railway finances and Leslie Bond, director of Rank Organisation, which had interests in motorway service stations. The Serpell Report, published in January 1983, put forward six proposals for the reduction of the BR deficit which if implemented would have amounted to the largest programme of cuts since Beeching. The Serpell Report proposed massive radical reductions in services and the closure of thousands of miles of rails, including a notorious 'Option A' which would have cut the railway network down to a minimum core of 1,600 miles. The report also recommended the running down of freight, the closure of services to ports, and the outsourcing of work from the engineering workshops.

The union responded to the Serpell Report with a mass campaign, in coordination with ASLEF and rail users' organisations. Transport 2000 published *Investing in British Rail* in June 1983 which directly contradicted most of the Serpell Report's findings. The NUR MPs launched sustained attacks on the report in the Commons. The government, stung by widespread public criticisms of its proposals, shelved most of Serpell's plans, but the BR board under Bob Reid embarked on radical reorganisation of the internal structure of BR, dividing it up into semi independent regional 'cost centres' and progressively hiving-off parts of the organisation which could be easily removed from the system. The Serpell Report had advocated the progressive dismemberment of its engineering workshops, the contracting out or sell-off of most core rail engineering and eventual closure of the BR workshops. In response to it BR and BREL management secretly agreed a policy of progressively running down its engineering arm, British Rail Engineering Limited (BREL).* The workshop closure programme fitted in with the government's plans to hive-off state industry to the private sector as BR began allocating new engineering work such as the construction of new Diesel Motor Units to BREL's competitors in the private sector such as Metro Cammell. BR's policy was to progressively run down the BREL workshops and help to build up its private sector competitors by gradually transferring new contracts for work allowing them to build up capacity.

The closure of the engineering workshops was one of the most spectacular acts of industrial vandalism of the 1980s. In the course of the mid 1980s BREL workshops at Swindon, Glasgow, Horwich, Shildon, Eastleigh and Derby were progressively run down and closed. In addition, dozens of smaller maintenance depots employing thousands of other workers were shut. Hardest hit were the historic railway towns that had developed around some of the earliest private engineering workshops of the steam era where the entire local economy, livelihood and local sense of identity were bound up with the railway industry. These communities, already hard hit by unemployment in other industries, were decimated by the loss of jobs.

In February 1983 news emerged of the closure of Horwich, near Bolton, with a loss of some 2,600 jobs and Temple Mills, Stratford, where over a thousand jobs were lost. Next to go were the workshops

---

* In May 1983 a leaked document revealed the BR/BREL agreed strategy: 'Radical manpower reductions will not arise solely because of reducing BR requirements, but also because of changing policies regarding BREL/Depots/ Private Sector. For this reason we firmly recommend that the situation should not be disclosed to the Unions, as it is felt the underlying reasons would bring severe industrial relations difficulties which would hinder the implementation of the plan', *Transport Review*, 25 May 1984.

at Shildon, County Durham, where 3,000 were employed. This town of 14,000 had developed around the workshops of the Lancashire and Yorkshire Railway where in the 1820s pioneer railway engineers Robert Stephenson and Timothy Hackworth developed some of the first locomotive engines. By the time of the closure of Shildon, Horwich and Temple Mills, British Rail was signalling that further closures at Swindon and Glasgow were looming. By the beginning of 1984 the spectre of privatisation was threatening the entire transport infrastructure. The NUR was gearing up for a period of prolonged trench warfare over the issue of workshop closures, new changes in working practices and threats to jobs.

> The works were the heart of the town. The Railway Institute and the pubs used to be packed at lunch time with shopmen. The union backed us up to the hilt when we fought to save them. We marched all over London. But Shildon was gutted. Six months after the works shut there were shutters going up everywhere, shops, pubs, the lot. I left with my family and found work at Eastleigh. We used to go back at weekends, but it was too much. I lost a few good mates. There were suicides. They just couldn't take it. Then Eastleigh was privatised. It was taken over by Alstrom in 1998. It was death by a thousand cuts. I took early redundancy before Eastleigh closed, to give one of the younger ones a better chance.
>
> Keith Erskine

## The Miners' Strike

In the midst of these disputes the Tories headed for confrontation with the miners. In March 1984 the National Coal Board announced the closure of Cortonwood colliery in South Yorkshire, followed by a shock announcement of a massive programme of further pit closures. In defiance of the recently passed 1984 Trade Union Act, which made pre-strike ballots compulsory, the NUM President Arthur Scargill won the backing of the NUM executive for a national coal strike. It was to be a year-long conflict in which the movement of coal, by rail, sea and road, was a critical factor.

The government and the National Coal Board were well prepared for the strike. Ever since Nicholas Ridley's 1978 paper on taking on the unions, secret plans had been laid for a successful confrontation with the miners, using military style policing, a concerted political and industrial campaign including secretly organising scabbing, the use of the law courts and orchestrated vilification of the miners by a compliant right wing press. Extensive plans to organise scab hauliers to bypass sympathy action by railwaymen and others were laid on. The reason for confronting the miners was obvious. The miners were identified as amongst the best organised and most militant of groups of workers in British industry. Their successful strike of 1974 had led directly to the downfall of the Conservative government of Edward Heath. Taking them on and winning was central to the Thatcherite project of breaking the power of the trade unions.

The miners were, by contrast, poorly prepared for the strike. The NUM were forced to strike at the beginning of spring, when stockpiles of coal, secretly built up by the government, were high and demand for fuel low. Much was made in the media of the lack of a ballot in direct defiance of Tory legislation. The failure to hold a vote made the NUM an easier target for a hostile press but as NUM national Vice-President Mick McGahey said at the time, 'how can it be right to vote someone else out of their job'. The cause of fighting for the preservation of jobs and communities in the face of the Thatcher government was without any doubt just, but with many in the Labour Party hierarchy as well as the TUC and other unions wishing to distance themselves from Arthur Scargill's militant stand, the trade union movement gave the miners half-hearted support. Led by Len Murray, the TUC was adopting a policy of adapting to rather than confronting directly the emerging Thatcherite consensus, a trend dubbed 'the new realism'. For its part the NUM did not seek the official support of the TUC, which it feared would seek to limit the impact of the strike, and sought instead to work directly with other sympathetic unions.

The lack of support from the Labour Party leadership and the TUC did not mean that individual unions and their members failed the miners' cause. At the outset of the strike the NUR and the NUS joined together with ASLEF, TSSA and the TGWU to coordinate their efforts. In mid March, just over a week after the strike began, the NUR national executive decided unanimously to 'affirm our full fraternal support for the mineworkers in their present struggle, and we will give sympathetic consideration for any request for assistance'. By late March, a transport coordinating committee was set up. It met throughout the strike at Unity House and Transport House. A potentially powerful alliance of the rail unions, along with the seafarers, dockers and steel workers was thus formed, though the ISTC later withdrew its support and the TGWU failed to prevent its members from driving scab lorries, or from preventing the handling of coal at docks after two dock strikes collapsed.

Despite this, railway workers and seafarers worked with others throughout the year-long strike to give support to the NUM. Over the twelve months of the strike the NUR and the NUS gave direct cash aid to the miners, financial support in interest free loans of hundreds of thousands of pounds. Both Jimmy Knapp of the NUR and Jim Slater of the NUS worked closely with the NUM during the strike, speaking countless times in support of the miners and attempting to coordinate a concerted campaign of solidarity. Knapp was a personal friend of NUM Vice-President Mick McGahey. Support for the miners came in the form of the twinning of NUR and NUS branches with pits, the setting up of miners support groups and the donation of thousands of pounds of cash. Railway workers and seafarers equally grasped the significance of the miner's struggle. Jim Slater, whose brother was a NUM member, recognised the threat posed by Thatcher's government should the strike be lost: 'we can't afford to let the miners lose this strike', he told one meeting during the early stages of the strike, 'it could put us back to 1926. And it is doubtful we could ever recover.'

Public solidarity and financial aid from the NUR and the NUS were less important than action on the ground. From the outset of the strike both unions instructed their branches to do all they could to stop the movement of coal. In coal depots and ports throughout the country individual NUR and NUS members blacked coal and in those parts of the country where support for the strike was solid not a ton of coal was handled. The seamen did all they could to help the strike, obstructed sea-borne shipments of coal and tried to persuade others not to scab. From the start of the strike NUS members refused to handle scab imported coal, and worked with the TGWU to stop its movement through the ports. Coal shipped coastwise from the North East was blacked by the NUS. In response the National Coal Board arranged for coal to be shipped in colliers and brought in through a myriad of small private harbours on the east coast. Jim Slater, who had served on a Polish ship during the war, appealed to the Polish Seamen's union not to handle scab coal but was told that the Polish ships were merely contracted to ship the coal to Amsterdam where it was then transferred to Dutch owned but out-flagged colliers.

> From day one our branches were told that no coal moves. Not a nugget. That's it. It was solid. Other sections of the union not directly involved in the movement of coal set up solidarity groups, like other unions, to sustain the miners financially. Our aim was to try to see that miners were not starved back.
>
> Geoff Revell

On land, support for the strike by NUR members in Scotland, South Wales, the North West, South Yorkshire and Kent was total. The turning point of the strike, the battle of Orgreave in the summer of 1984, was a direct result of the sympathetic blacking of coal movements by NUR members. Prior to the strike the giant Orgreave coking plant was entirely serviced by rail, with slack being moved in and reprocessed into coke which was transferred to important industrial sites such as the steel plant at Scunthorpe. The Tinsley branch of NUR and ASLEF members met with the NUM and agreed that if the miners mounted a picket over the road bridge at Treeton that rail workers would refuse to move trains in or out of the site. As a result the National Coal Board had to bring in coal by road, resulting in the Orgreave battle.

> I turned up for work that morning at half past seven. There was absolute chaos. There was everybody there. There were top managers. There were British Transport Police, civil police. The driver of the first train was prepared to take the coke train out and even the guard was prepared to take the train out but the shunter, a guy called Billy Burns, wouldn't open the point. Everybody got involved. And as a consequence of that the Local Departmental Committee of the union came up and gave a bollocking to the driver and the guard and from that day on not one single train moved in or out of Orgreave coking plant.
>
> Gerry Hitchen

Solidarity action took place wherever coal moved by rail, but in areas where the strike was less complete the membership was divided and the NUR members who supported the miners were subjected to a campaign of victimisation and intimidation. The two very different stories of solidarity action by railwaymen for the miners, at Coalville in Leicestershire and Shirebrook in Derbyshire, reveal the dilemmas faced by trade unionists in the midst of a struggle.

### 'The Men of Coalville'

As the name suggests, the Leicestershire town of Coalville was built around the mining industry. The Mantle Lane rail depot at Coalville was in the heart of the Leicestershire coalfields, and serviced three national power stations: Drakelow, Didcot and Rugeley. The Leicestershire coalfields were one of the centres of breakaway Spencer unionism during the 1926 General Strike, and this tradition persisted in the 1984 strike when some 2,500 miners worked on in defiance of the NUM. The NUR men of the Coalville depot, numbering over 160, took action in solidarity with the handful of NUM loyalists, dubbed 'the dirty thirty', who had joined the strike.

On 3 April 1984 NUR members at Coalville refused to handle the transport from the whole of the Leicestershire coalfields. When three guards were sent home, fellow railwaymen walked out. On 10 April a compromise was reached locally by which the NUR members agreed to move coal from a local privately owned open-cast mine in return for allowing the surplus men to continue on other duties. As a result virtually the whole of the coal worked from National Coal Board pits in Leicestershire was blacked, and for the first three months of the strike was stockpiled in huge heaps around the depot, testimony of the productivity of the working mines, but also the strength and solidarity of the railway workers.

As the strike headed towards summer, and the violent confrontations at Orgreave gave witness to the government's use of the police to break the strike, local BR management became more belligerent. On 7 June 1984 the regional operating manager ordered the men to resume normal working in 24 hours or face disciplinary action. Local branches of NUR and ASLEF stood firm and management responded by a lock out which lasted two months. Derbyshire branches of NUR and ASLEF went on a 24-hour strike in support of the Coalville men, closing the east coast main line. The management backed off for a time, apparently keen to limit any widening of the dispute into the railway industry, especially at the time of extensive national pay negotiations.

By the end of the summer, with pay negotiations settled, the attitude of BR changed. In late September a new area manager threatened to close the depot if the railwaymen did not return to work by 1 October. Perhaps not un-coincidentally, on the same day as the threat of closure was announced, British Transport Police raided homes of seven railwaymen, including the branch secretary, under suspicion of possessing railway property. Three were sacked after several items including soap, old cleaning rags and some batteries were found. More intimidation followed. In mid December 1984, when the National Coal Board was desperate to push the miners back to work and wanted to break the Coalville blockade, a signalman Edwin Hampton was declared 'mentally unstable' and moved to other work: a job sweeping platforms at Burton-on-Trent station. He was removed from his signal box for refusing to accept a management bribe to handle coal from a local pit to Drakelow power station. The Rail Federation of ASLEF and the NUR responded by calling for regional strike action at eleven depots covering the London Midland and Eastern regions of BR. On 17 January a 24-hour regional strike was held in freezing winter weather throughout the London Midland and Northeast regions of BR. Threatened with the extension of the strike to national level the management caved in.

## Struggle at Shirebrook

The coal depot at Shirebrook, north Derbyshire, which straddled the Nottinghamshire border, was also a site of bitter conflict. The situation here was more complicated than Coalville but equally intimidating. Close to the Nottinghamshire coalfields, one of the most hotly contested areas of the strike, Shirebrook depot serviced the nearby Shirebrook and Warsop collieries as well as eleven other mines in the area, operating a 'merry-go-round' service for the important electricity generating stations in the Trent valley: Ratcliffe-on-Soar, West Burton, High Marnham and Cottam. Though the men at the two local pits were behind the strike, in the surrounding countryside of north Nottinghamshire miners worked on. Loyalties were divided at the depot, with many men of the local branch having family connections with working miners. Local reluctance to join the action was explained by Dennis Widdowson, Branch Secretary at Shirebrook:

> 'my members have never disobeyed an executive instruction in the 19 years I have been branch secretary here. But they feel this isn't their fight, and it could jeopardise our industry... if the NUM held a national ballot, and got 55 per cent majority, and then decided to strike, of course my members would not move any coal.'

As a result only a handful of the NUR men initially took part in the action and some 75 NUR guards as well as ASLEF members worked on against the directive of both rail unions. From early April to the end of May 1984 six local branch meetings were held by union officials to persuade the men to act, but these efforts failed to resolve the issue. In June, Jimmy Knapp and Ray Buckton spoke to a joint meeting at Shirebrook and after what was described in *Transport Review* as a 'frank and open' debate, further 'very heated' local joint meetings were held, as Jimmy Knapp later recalled:

> 'They made it plain it was us they wanted to talk to. It was a very civilised meeting, no abuse. They raised all the natural questions. I had questions, for example, from a man who said he had two sons still digging coal. I spoke about the need to defend our industry and appealed basically to the loyalty of our members. In the 1980s you can't take that for granted; but the amazing thing is it did happen.'

As a result of these meetings a local vote of the Shirebrook men came out narrowly in support for the miners. By mid June, a third of the guards and more than half the drivers blacked coal movements. Further local lobbying by the NUR and ASLEF persuaded more men to join the action and by the height of the strike more than two-thirds of the guards and three-quarters of the drivers took part.

The crunch came in July, when the National Coal Board was embarked on an effort to force the miners at the local pits to get back to work. British Transport Police, in full riot gear with horses and dogs, were deployed in the depot. The police stopped and interviewed railwaymen on their way to work and set up in the very room in which the men clocked on. At the same time, local management at the depot suddenly refused to sign on anyone who refused to 'work normally', in other words to handle coal, and sent the men home. Those who blacked coal had 'Code 22' entered on their payslips which meant they were officially classed as on strike and so liable for no tax rebates. Management put up propaganda posters showing coal being moved by lorries and free visits were offered to railwaymen to see the convoys entering the power stations. Guards at Shirebrook and Warsop were phoned at home and cajoled and threatened to get them to resume coal movements. On 26 July the NUR and ASLEF threatened industrial action if the lock out continued. BR responded by appearing to make concessions and then almost immediately withdrawing them, as a way of getting the unions to call management's bluff. The strike threat was not carried out and the lock out continued over the summer. Finally in late September the NUR executive threatened industrial action if Shirebrook men continued to be intimidated. On 10 October NUR members went on a regional 24-hour strike in support of the Shirebrook depot.

The attitude of BR to the union during the strike was orchestrated behind the scenes by the Department of Transport which pursued a policy of making selective concessions so as not to aggravate the miners' strike into a wider industrial conflict. In the midst of the strike the NUR entered into the 1985 pay round. At first BR stuck to a tough negotiating position, a low offer of 4 per cent with significant 'efficiency savings', including driver only trains. But as the miners' strike continued, the Tories, fearing further industrial unrest, directed BR to back pedal and mollify the rail unions. In response to the initial 4 per cent offer the unions threatened an overtime and rest day ban from 30 May. The week before the start of the action the leaders of both unions were called in by BR Chairman Bob Reid and offered an improved 5.2 per cent, with 'no strings attached'.

The reasons for the BR climbdown were later revealed in a leaked letter, published by investigative journalist Paul Foot in the *Daily Mirror*, which detailed the government's tactic of making concessions to the rail unions. In one letter John Selwyn Gummer, Junior Environment Secretary and Tory Party Chairman, wrote to transport minister Nicholas Ridley that it was 'critical at this juncture to avoid the risk of militants being strengthened in their attempts to block the movement of coal by rail, and to make wider common cause with the miners'. The NUR and ASLEF accepted the new offer and the threatened action was called off. There was little room for a negotiating option. Under the McCarthy Tribunal formulae BR's new offer was its final negotiating position.

Despite the near total blockade on the railways, coal supplies continued to be moved by highly organised convoys of scab lorries. Road haulage contractors were happy to take advantage of the miners' strike, and the sight of convoys of coal sapped spirits. As the year 1984 ended there was the beginning of a concerted campaign to get the miners back to work, and the strike showed signs of faltering. By late November information began to filter in of a weakening of rank and file support. At Shirebrook the number of guards who were working normally returned to 50 per cent before Christmas. Though the blockade of coal continued into the new year the strike began to crumble. Sadly but with great dignity the miners returned to work at the beginning of March.

## The Aftermath of the Strike

> We were all gutted. Because the miners did everything. We knew what it was all about. We knew that the NUM was seen as the vanguard as far as the trade union movement was concerned. If they were defeated it would be a massive setback for us all. A lot of us had got family and friends who were very close to it all. South Yorkshire is a massive mining area, or it was. So we were all very closely involved, and very gutted about the way that it ended.
>
> Gerry Hitchen

The loss of the strike was a profound defeat for the organised labour movement in Britain, and had a direct impact not merely on the pit communities but on the whole of the industrial working class. The defeat demoralised trade union activists and divided the trade union movement. It demonstrated the raw power of the state to take on the most highly organised group of workers and win. There are those who argue it came about because the miners union had mistaken the political and industrial mood both of its own members and the wider trade union movement. Anything beyond limited solidarity action was not to be expected in an economic downturn; the government was too well prepared for the strike and the NUM's failure to call a ballot played into its hands. Others state that the strike's failure was down to the timidity of the trade union leadership and its unwillingness to take tougher action leaving the miners to fight alone.

> We had had many an argument in the cabin. You have got to understand the time: the whole propaganda machine was going, Thatcher was at her height. I think that had our leadership done what it should have done, along with the leaders of the other main trade unions, we wouldn't be sat here with all the problems we've got today.
>
> Gerry Hitchen

During and after the strike some NUR members criticised the national leadership for backing off from putting any pressure on BR at the time of the 1985 pay round and in general for failing to open up a 'second front' to help the miners win. In September 1986 Ayr branch thought that the climbdown on the 1985 wage claim was a serious error of judgement: 'At a time when we could have stood side by side with the miners and others, a better deal could have been obtainable – not only for us but for the miners too.' This criticism fed into wider dissatisfaction with the leadership's failure to take effective action against Thatcher's onslaught against the whole union movement.

Knapp later said: 'the miners never asked us to take strike action. I don't think feelings were ever strong enough for us to take that kind of action. What if we had tried it and got egg on our face? I don't think I would have called that action.' It was counter-argued that a widening of the strike, say by taking action which hit passenger services, would have helped to pile pressure on the government. But by 1985 this alone would have been unlikely to have tipped the balance in the miners' favour. There were too many other factors affecting the outcome of the strike, including the use of scab lorries, the lack of solidarity action by the energy and steel unions, the failure of the TGWU's port strikes and of the underestimated reluctance of the pit deputies union to go on strike, and not least the internal divisions within the miners' union itself. It must be said that everything the NUM asked from the NUR and the NUS in practical and financial terms they immediately got throughout the dispute. Despite twelve months of harassment the membership remained loyal to the miners. The instruction to the membership not

to move coal was issued at the commencement of the strike and not
lifted till requested by the NUM.

> An issue was how we used the wage settlements that were going on in
> the context of the miners' struggle. Nobody knew that the strike would
> go on for so long. When the miners went out that was when the wage
> settlements were going on. Lots of us wanted something to happen
> there and then. By the following February and March when things were
> gearing up and the miners had been out for some time there was an
> argument about the demands we were making. These debates have to
> be seen in the context of the NUM's position in the TUC, the role of
> other unions, it was not just the NUR and the NUS, all sorts of other
> unions were involved. On the docks Polish coal was coming in. Some
> of us wanted to open up a second front. There were those who were
> saying: look, we're losing jobs, we're losing people. That was the debate
> we were having.
>
> Geoff Revell

Regardless of the causes for the miners' defeat, the consequences
were directly felt by the transport industry. In the aftermath of the
strike the shift of freight from rail to road continued apace. Scargill's
predictions of widespread closures of pits proved all too true. These
had a knock-on effect on the coal depots. The heroic actions at Treeton,
Shirebrook, Coalville and elsewhere were rewarded with redundancies.
Within days of the strike ending there were eleven redundancies at
Coalville alone. Overall, hundreds of coal depot jobs were lost by the
NUR in the aftermath of the strike.

Nor was this all. BR management, emboldened by the crushing of the
miners, took full advantage of the demoralisation of railway workers
to push through a series of far reaching changes which the unions
were virtually powerless to prevent. In the wake of the strike BR and
LUL (London Underground Ltd) pressed on with the introduction
of driver only operations (DOO), with the threat to thousands of
NUR guards. One-man operation on sections of the East London and
District lines, hitherto confined to the Hammersmith and City line,
were proposed in spring 1985. On the day of imposition an all-out
strike without a ballot and against the law was called by the NUR

executive on London Underground and almost immediately collapsed (ASLEF accepted the imposition). In early June it was clear that BR Eastern Region was intent on foisting DOO on its workforce. Rather than negotiate these changes nationally, BR bypassed the NUR and attempted to persuade local and regional officials to accept DOO. This was followed by the snap announcement that BR intended to impose DOO on all passenger and freight trains in the network. In the wake of the miners' strike management felt strong enough to tear up agreed procedures, downgrading normal union contacts with BR from senior to middle managers.

The NUR attempted to adjust to the harsher post-strike atmosphere while trying to continue to press its demands. A key issue was whether to accept the implications of the new trade union legislation. Under Tory legislation passed in 1984 all unions were liable to ballot their members every four years on funding for political parties. The issue went to the heart of the historic links between the unions and the Labour Party, challenging the very right of trade unions to organise. NUR members were reminded of the time in the early history of the union, when during the Taff Vale dispute and the Osborne judgment the union had held ballots under legislation which overwhelmingly supported the financial backing of political activities. The foundation of the Labour Representation Committee and later the Labour Party, funded by trade unionists, was a direct result of the battle over political funds. A well-organised national campaign to support the political fund was mounted by the NUR and this succeeded in persuading the membership in backing the fund by a stunning majority of 87 per cent.

More controversially the national leadership, against some determined opposition, argued for the acceptance of the pre-strike ballot. Matters came to a head at the AGM held at Ayr in July 1985 when, after a hotly contested series of anti-ballot amendments were defeated, the meeting voted by 40 to 36 votes to ballot members in future before any strike action. Jimmy Knapp and others had argued that acceptance of the pre-strike ballot was a tactical move which would strengthen the hand of the union in any future dispute, and prevent it from having its funds sequestered by damaging court action. He said:

'At the moment they are using the ballot against us, like a sword hanging over our head. Let's grab that sword out of their hands and strike them with it! That is what they are afraid of more than anything else.'

Opponents of the pre-strike ballot saw the proposed change as a sell-out. The long history of trade union defiance of unjust laws was cited to show how the union should continue to resist the new legislation. As a delegate from Glasgow 12, H. Connolly, put it: 'if laws had not been broken in the past we wouldn't have a trade union movement. If you forget your past you betray your future.'

The logic of holding ballots and the mood of the union in the aftermath of the miners' strike was put to the test the following August when the NUR balloted members on taking action against DOO. In a blatant attempt to intimidate the membership in the midst of the ballot, BR sacked 200 guards from Immingham, Glasgow and south Wales for refusing to cooperate with DOO. The guards' leaders were outraged; the union had just agreed to abide by the law to ballot and now members had been sacked while conducting that ballot. The national executive faced a dilemma: should they cancel the strike ballot on DOO and call a ballot for strike action to defend the sacked guards, or let the ballot on DOO go ahead and build on the anger resulting from the dismissals? They decided on the latter and conducted meetings throughout the country to gain support. By a small majority of 500 the guards voted not to take action. It was a bitter blow for the union, though given the intimidation and the fact that the defeat of the miners had just taken place perhaps it should not have been surprising. A negotiating team was sent to the British Railways board to demand they immediately reinstate the sacked guards or face a further ballot for strike action. The BR negotiators set about humiliating the team by linking the reinstatements to promised progress on DOO, calling the guards 'your members, our previous employees'. Eventually all the sacked guards were given the offer of their jobs back without loss of service. Further defeats in pre-strike ballots were to follow. In May of the following year, as the progressive programme of closure of engineering workshops gathered pace, the NUR executive decided to call a ballot of workshop members for action. An extensive information campaign was mounted to publicise the plight of the shopmen and to make the case for action. A march and rally were held in London. Before the miners' strike BREL had closed or run down Shildon and Horwich and threatened Swindon and Glasgow. Now the threat was widened to a hit list of some 16 smaller regional repairing and maintenance workshops, such as the tiny Toton Wagon shop which employed a mere 39 shopmen, as well as the threat of redundancies at a further 20 sites, including large-scale losses at Glasgow, Eastleigh, Doncaster and Swindon. In all some 8,000 jobs were under immediate threat, with no guarantee that more job losses would not follow. The ballot, conducted on 30 June 1986, was conclusive. Strike action was not adopted by some 11,700 votes against, with less than 6,000 votes for. The defeats in the strike ballots signalled that a demoralised workforce, who had just witnessed another group of workers go to the wall after a year-long national strike, was in no position to take on management.

---

There was a certain pessimism that nobody could win if the miners couldn't win. That was exactly the message that Thatcher was trying to put out. At first, with the whole anti-union legislation there was a general feeling that can we ever win a secret ballot because of the interference of the press and media. The legislation was so weighted against us. We saw the NUM having its assets sequestrated. But we fairly quickly overcame it. We were one of the first unions to start winning ballots for strikes. To a certain extent we set the trend for other unions. We certainly have no fear now.

Gerry Hitchen

---

Demoralisation brought decline: by the end of the 1980s the number of workers who belonged to trade unions hovered just above 30 per cent of the adult male workforce. Weakened trade unions made it easier for employers and the Tories to push forward their plans for privatisation. The field was open for a new wave of sell offs, especially in transport. Within the wider movement the defeat of the miners helped reinforce the position of the so-called 'new realists', associated with TUC General Secretary Norman Willis, who argued that trade unionists had to work within rather than resist the changing legal framework of industrial relations. The defeat led to a growing acceptance among trade unionists and the Labour Party of the unfeasibility of repealing *all* the Tory anti-trade union legislation, rather than the most onerous laws. More popular measures, such as ballots for executive elections and before strikes, were to be retained. It was upon this basis that Labour fought and lost the 1987 general election. Labour's third defeat by the Tories led to further anti-union laws and strengthened the position of the 'new realists' in the union movement. Faced by continued electoral defeat, the trade unions and the Labour Party moved further to the right. Some saw this as a strategic reorientation of the movement to the realities of the late 1980s, a necessary task of modernisation. For others this was retreat before the class enemy, a gross betrayal of the movement's core principles. The scars of the 1984–85 strike would take many years to heal.

# 4
# Turning the Corner

## After the Miners' Strike: the Position of Both Unions

THE MINERS' DEFEAT USHERED IN a period of retrenchment and retreat. Years were to pass before workers regained the confidence to take on the employers, who were encouraged by the strike's failure to impose new tough management regimes. In the aftermath of the strike the government sped up its twin policies of privatisation and anti-union legal reform. Reeling from the body blow inflicted by the defeat, the NUR and the NUS sought to adjust to the bleaker industrial relations of the late 1980s, working within and around the new Tory legislation. In the case of the NUR, successive setbacks were to be suffered but the union began to turn the corner at the end of the 1980s. The NUS was not so lucky: after a period of resistance it fought and lost a year-long dispute with P&O, which broke the back of the union. Both organisations undertook successful ballots for industrial action under the new laws but then fell foul of the courts.

New Tory legislation introduced in the aftermath of the strike further narrowed the rights of unions and limited their room to manoeuvre. The new laws, presented to the public as a means of redressing the rights of individual workers in relation to the unions and for protecting society at large from damaging and disruptive strikes, were in fact a way of limiting the ability of unions to take collective action in relation to employers through crippling injunctions while at the same time whittling

away at the unions' membership base. In 1986 the Employment Bill
was published: this bill which became law in 1988 further eroded
the closed shop, by making it easier for employers and members to
take legal action against unions; especially part 2 which amounted
to a 'scab's charter'. The 1988 Employment Act limited the closed
shop, banned unions from disciplining strike-breaking members, and
made postal votes for elections and strike ballots mandatory. The 1990
Employment Act outlawed the pre-entry closed shop and secondary
picketing and made unions financially liable for wildcat strikes. Finally
the 1993 Trade Union Reform and Employment Rights Act abolished
the Wages Councils (which set wage minimums in several industries),
ended automatic deduction or 'check off' of union dues and brought
in the right of members to join the union of their choice (undermining
the Bridlington Agreement which stopped unions poaching each other's
members).

New legislation further eroded the position of publicly owned
transport networks and paved the way for future privatisations
affecting the transport sector. The Tories' victory over the miners
hastened the privatisation of transport with the passage of the 1985
Transport Act, which came into law in October 1986. This led to an
extension of privatisation to municipal bus services, with notorious
results; 'Deregulation Day' on the buses led to traffic snarl-ups in major
towns and cities as competing bus services lined up. The National Bus
Company (NBC) was fragmented into some 70 constituent companies.
New, independently owned bus firms such as Brian Souter's Stagecoach
took over many services and after an initial period of chaos with a huge
number of small competitors for urban bus services several larger firms
came to the fore. As a result national wages agreements were effectively
torn up as transport unions had to enter into separate negotiations
with individual companies.* The significance of the privatisation of
the NBC was that the same principles of competition were later to be
so inappropriately applied to the railways. It also created some of the
new private transport companies which would eventually bid for rail
services. The years after the strike saw the heyday of a new buccaneering
type of international capitalism, dominated by big conglomerates
acquiring international interests in engineering, property, railways,

---

* The NUR's 6,500 busmen's section joined with the four other bus unions to
  create a united front with which to enter into negotiations.

shipping and port facilities. This was also the era of a North American-inspired 'hard ball' management style, with the rise of a new type of intransigent senior manager, often brought in from outside industries with experience of taking on unions and defeating them.

> After the miners strike management strutted. There was no doubt about it at all. You used to have the negotiating committee go over to meet the BR board. We'd been used to sitting around the table with the bosses from each of the regions, with their expensive clothes and their secretaries with them, chaired by the one man down from the chairman of the board. On many occasions the Chairman of British Rail would be present in the room. I remember going over then, after the miners' strike, and there were these wide boys, these underlings and gofers, sitting across the table from the General Secretary of our union. It was a signal. That came to a head when they sacked the guards at Immingham and Glasgow. They would openly sit there and sneer at us. Bob Crow remembers when the 'Company Plan' was introduced on London Underground, that we were told 'in ten years time there won't be any unions'. Of course they were wrong big time. We never took it lying down. We weren't going anywhere.
>
> Geoff Revell

## The NUS: 'Left to Bleed to Death on the Altar of Free Trade'

For the seamen the years after the miners' strike were marked by a devastating haemorrhage of jobs. The position of the union became critical in the second half of the 1980s. By 1987, the centenary of its foundation, it had only 24,000 members, down from 60,000 in 1980. The worldwide slump in demand for shipping, which began in the early 1980s, continued as Britain's merchant fleet dwindled to a mere 600 ships by 1988. The big shipping lines rushed to divest themselves of British registration. The parlous situation of British shipping, and by implication of the NUS, was summed up by Sam McCluskie in his speech delivered at the September 1987 celebrations of the NUS centenary: 'A great industry and great maritime tradition are being left to bleed to death at the altar of free trade.' The following year the NUS found itself drawn into a long and bitter strike that was to effectively break the finances if not the spirit of the hundred year old union.

These years were characterised by buy-outs of shipping and port facilities by international property and construction firms such as Trafalgar House, which took over Cunard in 1980, and P&O, the great survivor of British maritime history, which merged in 1987 with the property and financial services group Sterling Guarantee Trust. Independent shipping lines serving ports gave way to integrated conglomerates which managed port facilities, haulage and inland distribution points but also had interests in construction, property and commercial and financial services. The period saw the growth of so-called 'Offshore Registers', such as the Isle of Man, which were nominally part of the national register of shipping but exempted from UK labour laws. Firms like Shell transferred dozens of ships to offshore registration in the second half of the 1980s. The prolonged slump in world deep-sea shipping also saw the disappearance of cargo liners and the flagging out or scrapping of the UK's bulk cargo, oil and gas tankers. Without government aid UK shipbuilding became confined largely to the construction of naval ships. One bright spot was the North Sea oil industry, where there was an increasing demand for service vessels.

Britain's share of the world's deep-sea shipping spiralled downwards as shorter European routes took on greater importance. As a result traffic on the cross-Channel ferries, carrying both tourists and freight, grew in significance, generating demand for roll-on roll-off ships of increasing size. The privatisation of Sealink in 1983, which was taken over by Sea Containers Ltd, and the beginning of construction of the Channel tunnel in 1986, enhanced the breakneck competitiveness of the cross-Channel ferry market. The conglomerate P&O took over Sealink's leading competitor Townsend Thoresen in January 1987 and became the largest employer of unionised seamen in the UK. Led by its new Chairman Jeffrey Sterling, a close confidant of Margaret Thatcher and special adviser to the Department of Trade and Industry, P&O European Ferries sought to reduce costs in the run up to the completion of the Channel tunnel by implementing a major restructuring of its Dover based cross-Channel services. At the same time Sterling signalled his intention to pull out of Townsend Thoresen's route sharing agreement with its rival Sealink. The new company was going to try to dominate the lucrative cross-Channel market. The rush for profits on the Channel ferries may have indirectly contributed to the worst peacetime maritime disaster since the sinking of the *Titanic*. Shortly after 5pm on 6 March 1987 the British registered roll-on roll-off ferry *Herald of Free Enterprise* capsized in the mouth of Zeebrugge harbour after leaving port with its bow doors open. 193 passengers and crew were lost, including 33 NUS members. The official inquiry into the disaster under Lord Justice Sheen pointed to poor management, 'the disease of sloppiness', as the primary cause of the disaster.

### The P&O Dover Strike: 'The Seamen's Wapping'

The first formal negotiations meeting between representatives of the NUS and P&O took place on 16 October 1987, ten months after the acquisition of Townsend Thoresen and more than six months after the Zeebrugge disaster. The old collective bargaining agreement with Townsend Thoresen, negotiated under the National Maritime Board, was due to expire at the beginning of 1988. P&O Chairman Jeffrey Sterling stressed that the company was going to take on its main ferry competitor, Sealink, and would be seeking to make significant changes to manning requirements and work organisation on the Dover ferries in anticipation of the opening of the Channel tunnel in 1993. At the same time Sterling gave an undertaking that any changes to be made would be introduced gradually and through negotiation with the NUS. This promise was broken in early December when P&O peremptorily announced a wholesale programme of layoffs, the reduction of manning levels and loss of between £35 and £45 weekly overtime pay, an increase in working hours from 12 to 16 hours, the replacement of day on/day off with a weekly shift of 168 hours and the loss of 10 days paid leave per year. In all Sterling was seeking to reduce P&O's wages bill at Dover by some £6 million per year. Over 2,000 seamen, more than a third of the NUS ferry membership, were affected and some 400 men stood to lose their jobs immediately when the new scheme was introduced in March 1988.

The snap announcement shocked the Dover NUS members and led to a hardening of the mood at the port. Despite calls for industrial action the union opted to enter negotiations with P&O to see if the company's cost-cutting programme could be modified. Meanwhile the Isle of Man Steam Packet Company, which plied Irish Sea routes, decided to lay off 70 seamen and impose new contracts entailing a reduction of 52 days annual leave on its crews. At the same time the company announced its intention to follow the policy of the deep-sea freight and cruise lines by leaving the existing Merchant Navy Establishment and the National Maritime Board, freeing it of a responsibility of employing British seamen. The prospect of the flagging out of the UK ferry fleet, one of the last bastions of unionised seamen, loomed on the horizon. New contracts were sent out to some 161 NUS members who were sacked when they refused to sign. The NUS called a local strike on 29 December 1988 but when negotiations failed to make any headway the union's executive took the fateful decision to widen the action. The National Ferry Port Committee of the union was called together and voted to stage a nationwide 24-hour ferry strike in support of the Isle of Man strikers and in protest against the tearing up of existing agreements and flagging out.

On 31 January 1988 some 7,000 NUS members staged a nationwide strike. The action was officially set to last for only 24 hours but extended into the first two days of February. P&O and Sealink immediately sought and were granted injunctions against the NUS for its failure to hold a lawful ballot under the 1984 Trade Union Act. At the same time the High Court ruled that the union was in contempt of the 1980 Employment Act for staging a form of illegal secondary action and was therefore liable to fines and sequestration. Though the union leadership initially argued that the nationwide strike was a legitimate response to a concerted attack by the ferry operators on existing working agreements and that mass meetings at the ferry ports had endorsed strike action by a show of hands, it backed down in the face of the threat of fines and sequestration. The High Court had fined the union some £7,500 and ordered it to pay £100,000 in legal costs. The NUS executive called off the strike, but many of the rank and file, especially the Dover men engaged in the simmering dispute with P&O, refused to come off the picket lines. P&O suspended negotiations on new contracts when the nationwide strike began and by the morning of 2 February, as the rest of the NUS ferry crews returned to work, some 2,300 seamen at Dover voted to take strike action against P&O from 3 February.*

---

* Ironically, given that the injunctions granted to P&O and Sealink would later be used to sequester the union's assets, the dispute with the Isle of Man Steamship Company was settled through ACAS. The company agreed to limit redundancies to 47 jobs, leave existing conditions in place and postpone its plan to leave the Merchant Navy Establishment.

Faced with a legally balloted strike action P&O agreed to talks with the NUS, though subsequent events were to demonstrate the intransigence and bad faith of the company. Negotiations were held four times between late February and early March as P&O's ships at Dover stood idle. Face to face talks broke down and the two parties went to ACAS. It became clear to the Dover seamen that P&O would not budge on its basic demand for a £6 million savings and something like between 260 and 360 redundancies and substantial changes to pay and conditions. A mass meeting at Dover decided to continue strike action. P&O responded on 16 March by issuing individual ten-day notices of dismissal unless the union agreed to sign up to new contracts. At the same time P&O threatened that after 23 March it would resort to non-union foreign labour.

The effective threat to flag out the P&O ferry fleet galvanised the rank and file. Across the country NUS shop stewards demanded national strike action in support of the Dover members. The union then called a national ballot and on 22 March posted ballots for return by the end of the month. Though provoked by the Dover strike the ballot was called on the national issues of job cuts, flagging out and changes in working practices throughout the UK ferry industry. NUS lawyers hoped that the terms of the ballot, on industry wide issues, would not be taken in court to violate the law on secondary picketing. This optimistic view had not reckoned with the intransigence of P&O, nor with the willingness of the courts to intervene in favour of employers. P&O applied to Justice Davies for an injunction against the union and in a strikingly dubious interpretation of the law on secondary action Justice Davies ruled that the terms of the ballot were 'an ingenious and ingenuous attempt to get around the law'. The judge granted an injunction prohibiting the ballot from going ahead while the 21,000 ballots were still in the post, on the tenuous basis that the outcome of the vote might result in secondary action. Faced with the prospect of further fines, the NUS announced that any returned ballots would remain unopened. In the late 1980s it seemed there were few ways to conduct industrial action and not fall foul of the law. One NUS member was reported to have remarked, 'why don't the Tories have done with it and make all strikes illegal'.

The suspension of the ballot brought a brief respite for the union. Talks between the NUS and P&O via ACAS resumed and the company produced what it called two new options involving 260–360 redundancies plus new work rotas extending hours and cutting overtime. A mass meeting at Dover on 3 April rejected both options and P&O responded by withdrawing from the ACAS talks. Support for the Dover strikers came from the officers' union NUMAST, whose 600 Dover based members voted on 8 April to work only with NUS crews. P&O then tried the tactic, perfected during the miners' strike, of directly approaching individual NUS members to persuade and cajole them back to work. Individual letters were sent out by P&O on 15 April with another 'new' offer (a slight improvement on basic pay with little change from earlier proposals). The offer was strictly time limited and would only apply to those men who accepted by 6pm of the fifth day after the offer was made. The tactic partially worked. Though another mass meeting at Dover voted by a show of hands to reject the new offer, some 1,000 strikers went back to work by the time the company's offer expired.

The push back to work began in earnest, and served to harden P&O's stance and the bitterness of the pickets at Dover. On 25 April P&O moved rapidly, announcing the de-recognition of the NUS and its intention to pull out of the Merchant Navy Establishment. Advertisements for strike breakers were placed in the newspapers. The union responded by mounting mass pickets of the Dover docks while trying to turn the tables on P&O by taking it to court. Not unsurprisingly an injunction against the company preventing it from withdrawing recognition failed while the call for mass pickets left the union wide open for legal action. Slowly but inexorably support for the strike began to crumble. Though only about 300 pickets turned out each day at the end of April this was enough to persuade some of the NUS crews on Sealink ferries not to cross the picket line which prevented two of its ships from sailing. This widened the strike once again but made the NUS liable to court action by Sealink on the basis of a breach of an earlier injunction against secondary action. Behind the scenes negotiations took place between NUS officials and Sealink management to see if court action could be averted by calling off the mass picketing of Sealink ships in return for the company acting as a go-between for the NUS and P&O. Sealink boss James Sherwood gave a promise to work with the union to see if the two ferry companies could come up with an industry-wide manning arrangement. These negotiations came to nothing and the NUS secondary action against Sealink resumed, thus placing the union on a direct collision course with the courts. Direct attempts to talk to P&O on the basis of significant concessions by the union were rebuffed by management. A meeting between Sam McCluskie, Jim Slater and Jeffrey Sterling at P&O's Pall Mall office took place on the evening of 29 April but it yielded no progress. In a move reminiscent of the tactics of nineteenth century strike breaking, P&O arranged for scab crews to man two of its vessels stranded at Rotterdam to sail back to Dover on 30 April. The NUS responded by what was seen as one last great effort to mobilise solidarity action across the industry. Through telex messages to all ships around the world flying the red duster General Secretary Sam McCluskie called for international strike action.

On 1 May, amidst angry pickets at the dock entrance, P&O managed to get its first ferry out of Dover harbour for three months. The *Pride of Bruges* sailed using a mixed crew of strike breakers and men who had previously been on strike. Two days later in the High Court Justice Davies ordered the sequestration of NUS assets and a £150,000 fine for 'flagrantly, repeatedly and gravely' continuing secondary pickets against Sealink in defiance of the earlier injunction. Justice Davies called the union's action 'attempted suicide' but it was clear that P&O was intent on destroying the union. Maritime House in south London, plus the union's offices at Dublin, Belfast, Aberdeen and Glasgow and elsewhere were taken over by officials appointed by the court.* Staff pay was stopped and the union's assets were frozen. The NUS took to meeting elsewhere; at the Prince of Wales pub across from Maritime House, at the nearby offices of the construction workers' union ACATT and in premises provided by local Labour Party branches and trades councils. As the sequestrators moved into Maritime House Sam McCluskie pledged continuing defiance: 'They can take our money... but they can't take our dignity.'

McCluskie's call for continuing action in the face of sequestration was answered up and down the country. Ferries stood idle throughout the UK. North Sea oil supply vessels joined in. At Aberdeen 2,000 seafarers working in the North Sea oil industry took action in support

---

* At Aberdeen NUS members occupied their headquarters and defied the sequestrators when they learned that the court orders from London were not immediately valid in Scotland.

of their fellow workers at Dover. Calls to French and Dutch dockers' unions met with some response, though officials at Rotterdam pointed to the fact that TGWU dockers at Dover continued to work on. A short-lived blockade of the port entrance by lorry drivers at first seemed like a widening of the action but soon evaporated. Secondary action, particularly with regard to Sealink, was difficult to maintain and left the union liable to yet more legal action. Talks at ACAS between Sealink and the NUS, aimed at lifting action against it in return for an agreement by Sealink to employ 450 of the remaining 743 P&O ferrymen still out on strike, were rejected by a mass meeting at Dover. After 14 weeks on strike the Dover strike committee was understandably reluctant to see any of the remaining strikers left out in the cold. But support for secondary action against Sealink began to rapidly fall apart after its chairman indicated that it too would leave the Merchant Navy Establishment if the dispute was not settled. Mr Justice Davies ratcheted up the screws by imposing a further £150,000 fine for the union's continuing defiance of the injunction against secondary action.

Faced with these onslaughts the union climbed down. On 12 May the NUS executive, meeting at Hull prior to the union's bi-annual general meeting, voted to call off all secondary action. Delegates to the Hull conference angrily denounced the decision, though motions from Liverpool and Harwich calling on the executive to resign were heavily defeated. The lifting of secondary action meant the union had purged its contempt of the injunction and could expect to see sequestration lifted. But within days of the union's decision P&O rushed back to the High Court and sought a further ruling against the union on the basis that the union was engaged in 'intimidatory' mass pickets. On 24 May Justice Davies sided once again with P&O and ruled that the sequestration of the union's assets should continue, even though the injunction had been granted to Sealink on a completely separate legal issue. By this stage the pickets had dwindled to as few as 150–200 men. Under the 1984 Act the Department of Employment had laid down a 'picketing code', which specified a maximum of six pickets and this figure had been used in the High Court since the 1986 News International dispute.

Three days after the judge's ruling a mass meeting at Dover voted to continue picketing. P&O stated that it 'regarded the dispute as over. All the people who didn't want to work for us have left and we have recruited virtually everyone else we need.' Though picketing continued and the sequestration order remained in place the union tried desperately to get back in control of its assets while maintaining the strike action. Faced with the threat of a further £150,000 fine the union set up a separate six-man picket in order to comply with the letter of the law, and the national executive officially disassociated itself from the continuing mass pickets. But the High Court held the sequestration order in place and rejected the union's application to return control of its assets. At last Judge Davies ruled that sequestration would be lifted after a probationary period and the payment of a further £25,000 fine. In early June the remaining P&O strikers, now down to a mere 227 men, voted to end their action. On 15 August 1988 the sequestration order was lifted. The strike had cost the union approximately £1.5 million in fines and legal fees out of assets, excluding Maritime House, of £2.6 million. Its membership, which stood at more than 24,000 at the start of the strike, was hovering below 20,000. The strike cost P&O some £40 million out of annual profits of the parent company of over £300 million. A mighty multinational corporation had used the full weight of the law to break up a trade union. The union founded by Havelock Wilson and the seamen of the north east just a hundred years previously was nearly bankrupt.

## The NUR after the Miners' Strike

Emboldened by the crushing of the miners, BR management took full advantage of the demoralisation of railway workers to push through a series of far reaching changes which the union was at first virtually powerless to prevent. In the wake of the strike management felt strong enough to tear up agreed procedures, downgrading normal union contacts with BR from senior to middle managers. British Rail and London Underground pressed on with the introduction of driver only operations (DOO), with the threat to thousands of NUR guards. The NUR held successive failed ballots for industrial action over the issue of DOO on British Rail and London Underground, as well as in defence of the shopmen in 1985–86.

The result of the failed ballots was to encourage management to go even further in their plans to 'streamline' the industry. Core parts of BR were split up and subject to rigid cost cutting. In 1986, under the so-called 'Trainman' concept, a new grade of multi-functional trainman/woman replaced the grades of driver's assistant, relief driver and guard. Thousands of jobs were lost by the introduction of the 'Open Station' concept which left stations without staff for large parts of the day leading to increases in vandalism and violence against passengers. Automatic ticket barriers on London Underground and new computerised ticketing systems led to widespread job losses.

The defeats of the mid 1980s also led to the final agony of the railway workshops. The failure of strike ballots in 1986 resulted in the closure of Swindon, the birthplace of the Great Western Railway, closed down in 1986 with the loss of 14,000 jobs. The site was sold to Tarmac. A town whose entire modern history was based around the railways was devastated. Unemployment there rose to 18 per cent and within a few years the small West Country railway town bore all the hallmarks of urban industrial decay with its attendant social ills. Similar stories occurred at Doncaster, sold in May 1987 to a management buyout trading as RFS industries. The Horwich Foundry was later separately sold to a castings firm. BREL itself after much financial chicanery was privatised in April 1987 when it passed to a consortia consisting of the engineers Asea Brown Boveri, Trafalgar House and BREL's own management team.* The closure of the BR workshops in historic railway towns such as Shildon, Horwich and Swindon sacrificed entire communities, with working class traditions going back generations, to the gods of the market. The progressive break-up of British Rail was all but inevitable, and it became a question not of if but how and when.

## 'Action 1989'

Yet despite these setbacks, by the end of the 1980s the tide began to turn. When Thatcher won a third electoral victory in 1987 railway workers began to recover the collective will to challenge the government and the employers. Ballots for action under the new legislation began to be won. In October 1986 a ballot of NUR members involved in a dispute with Sealink over Isle of White services produced a big yes vote. In January 1987 the NUR staged a successful ballot for action on the London Underground over the issue of competitive tendering

---

* Asea Brown Boveri later bought out Trafalgar House and in 1992 the company was renamed ABB transportation and became part of the multinational Adtranz group.

and the impact of new ticketing systems. The threatened strike was suspended after LUL agreed to negotiate with the union. In June of 1988 a ballot of signals and traffic members produced a large majority against BR's imposition of a new pay and grading structure. BR's official staff magazine had actively urged members to take part in the ballot, believing a high turnout would produce a 'no' vote. Armed with this resounding endorsement for strike action the executive called an overtime ban and, withholding the strike as a bargaining tool, forced BR back to the negotiating table, winning significant concessions on the new grading structure. This minor victory presaged a newfound self-confidence.

On London Underground a new mood of defiance arose in response to management attempts to implement a major programme of structural reorganisation and cost savings following the disastrous Kings Cross fire of November 1987. Thirty-one people died, including several station staff, when a smouldering fire caused by a dropped smoker's match was allowed to grow to a fireball which enveloped the main ticket hall. The official inquiry into the fire led by Desmond Fennell QC revealed a series of management failures and lax standards. Fennell in particular pointed to the complacent atmosphere of LUL safety procedures, which involved only a minimum amount of training for station staff. The LUL managing director, Tony Ridley, who had been pursuing a policy of shedding station staff before the fire and continued to do so after it despite union demands to halt the job cuts, came off particularly badly in the Fennell report and resigned directly after its publication in November 1988. Dennis Tunnicliffe, a former BA pilot and part of the notoriously anti-union British Airways management team led by Lord King, replaced him. Tunnicliffe took the opportunity provided by the Fennell report to attempt a complete overhaul of LUL management and push ahead with the so-called 'Company Plan' which involved a wholesale de-layering of LUL staff, including 5,000 redundancies among frontline staff including platform assistants and track maintenance crews. In addition to this, Tunnicliffe sought to bring in a new accelerated promotion structure for specially chosen prospective management trainees, dubbed 'Action Stations', bypassing LUL's traditional system of promotion on the basis of seniority and set exams. Defended by Tunnicliffe as a means of rewarding talent it was seen by the union as an assault on existing grades and the job

prospects of its members and as a means of creating an inner cadre of
management loyalists amongst junior staff, 'blue eyed boys', who would
be elevated above the rank and file. For LUL's West Indian and Asian
staff, many of them recruited in the 1960s and 1970s, the prospect
of being denied promotion on seniority after years of service seemed
particularly unfair. There was no doubt that in the wake of the King's
Cross fire LUL had to change, but it soon became evident that laying
behind the Company Plan was an assault on the rights of Underground
workers and the position of the union which represented them. A
ballot for action against Tunnicliffe's 'Action Stations' produced an
overwhelming seven to one vote in favour of industrial action. Like the
seafarers' union, the NUR was hauled up before the full panoply of the
law courts. LUL management used the Tory anti-strike laws to stifle
the action. On 25 April 1989 LUL were informed of the outcome of
the ballot and that a strike would start on 7 May. At 11am on 3 May
LUL gave notice that unless they heard by noon of the same day that
the strike would be called off, they would apply for an injunction that
afternoon. With just three hours to prepare a legal defence the union
went through a rushed hearing at the High Court. Justice Simon Brown,
though expressing some consternation at LUL's legal tactics, ruled that
the wording of the questions on the ballot paper gave sufficient cause
to grant an injunction against the NUR requiring it to call off the
strike. Jimmy Knapp told a press conference: 'we are rapidly reaching
the position in this country where it is not possible to call a strike and
remain within the law'. The union held a second ballot, with more
precise wording which produced a similar majority for strike action.
This time it went unchallenged. A mood of militancy arose on the
Underground in response to Tunnicliffe's new regime that set the stage
for the coming industrial action in the metropolis that would feed into
a wider, nationwide strike wave.

Behind the resurgence of rank and file activism lay concern over
wages. By the late 1980s comparative rates of pay for railway workers
were falling behind equivalent jobs in other industries. The basic weekly
pay of a railway worker in 1975 was £33.35 per week, by 1989 it was
£105.30, a reduction in real terms of some 6 per cent which contrasted
sharply with other workers. Low basic rates of pay on the railways
were supplemented by overtime: by the late 1980s conciliation staff
were averaging more than 50 hours per week. The retention of earnings

in the form of overtime had been behind the flexible rostering disputes of the early 1980s, and the national negotiating mechanisms had been the union's frontline of defence of wages in a period of inflation. Bargaining on pay and conditions through bodies such as the Local District Committees (LDCs) and the Rail Staffs National Tribunal was to the uncompromising management of BR of the late 1980s an unnecessary and burdensome hangover from the past. BR's new managing director of personnel, Trevor Toolan, who had been brought into BR by Sir Bob Reid (not to be confused with his predecessor in the post of the same name) after a period of union busting at Land Rover, epitomised the more hard-nosed Thatcherite approach to industrial relations. His new macho management regime was egged on by the more Thatcherite members of the BR board and the Department of Transport. Having effectively tried to cut out the white-collar union TSSA from national negotiating on pay and conditions by introducing individual contracts he sought to do something similar to the main rail unions.

In the autumn of 1988 British Rail proposed scrapping traditional national collective bargaining procedures by getting rid of the LDCs and sectional councils and devolving negotiations down to the local level so as to sap the union's national negotiating strength. In November 1988 the BR board gave statutory twelve months' notice of intent to change the negotiating procedures. Union dismay at this change was compounded by BR's miserly stance on pay, which was set below inflation increases at between 6.7 and 7 per cent for the 1989–90 pay claim at a time when inflation was running at 7.4 per cent. Matters came to a head after six weeks of intense negotiations in the spring of 1989. In March the BR board stated that its decision to abandon nationwide negotiations was 'irreversible'. In response the NUR executive decided on 5 May to ballot members on industrial action on the twin issues of the pay claim and the scrapping of national collective bargaining. ASLEF, as part of the Rail Federation, opted to hold a simultaneous ballot. BR responded by informing the unions on 9 May of its intention of imposing 7 per cent on pay without reference back to the Rail Staffs National Tribunal.

BR's handling of the dispute was cack-handed and disingenuous. The decision to ballot for industrial action was taken by the NUR executive in early May and letters of notification were sent to the

British Rail board with requests for facilities for holding a vote as mandated by legislation. But at the end of May with just a week to go before the vote the BR director of employee relations Paul Watkinson wrote to Jimmy Knapp telling him that he was surprised to learn of the proposed ballot as 'in the view of the Board no dispute currently exists', claiming that the union had repeatedly failed to discuss new negotiating procedures – this coming after the BR board had earlier stated that its position on the procedures was irreversible. The union suspected that objections to the ballot were intentionally being raised so close to the date of the vote with court action in mind. These suspicions were later to prove correct.

## 'See You in Court'

Balloting took place over five days from 30 May to 3 June. In the run up to the vote the membership were bombarded with letters and leaflets promising more money in some instances, threatening redundancies in others. Local managers interviewed individual members to persuade them not to vote to strike. In the immediate run up to the ballot BR dangled an extra £18 million for wage increases in London and the South East region. Despite this NUR members in London and the South East held solid and when the ballot result was announced in mid June there was overwhelming support for industrial action. The first of six 24-hour rail strikes, the first national rail strike for ten years, was called for 21 June, mid-summer's day. The strike call apparently had a salutary effect on BR management which hurriedly went to ACAS and invited the union to talks. Jimmy Knapp and the NUR negotiating team arrived at ACAS at 1.30 pm on the Friday before the strike. Thirty minutes into the talks a message was passed into the meeting room telling Knapp that a representative from BR wanted to see him and the chief officer of ACAS. Once outside he was told that BR would be seeking an injunction against the union to halt the strike. BR's director of employee relations and its chief negotiator at the ACAS talks, Paul Watkinson, expressed total surprise at news of the injunction, claiming to have only heard of it that day from the managing director of personnel Trevor Toolan.

BR's plea for an injunction to stop the strike was heard before Justice Vinelott on the following Monday morning. BR's case was feeble.

Though the union had been scrupulous in following the letter of the law on strike ballots, BR's lawyers claimed that the vote was invalid because a very small number of members (far fewer than voted in favour of action) had not received ballot papers. Paul Watkinson's position was totally undermined when his affidavit was submitted in court dated the previous Tuesday, 13 June, four days before he claimed to have first heard that BR would be taking legal action. After hearing arguments from both sides the judge ruled against BR, claiming that its evidence did not 'come anywhere near' justifying an injunction: 'a ballot cannot be invalid just because it proves impractical to contact someone on leave or bring a member from his sick bed'. Throwing out BR's case the judge ruled that the NUR had presented an 'impressive body of evidence' to justify its claim that the ballot was valid in law. The next day BR immediately went to the court of appeal where Lord Donaldson upheld Justice Vinelott's ruling against BR and awarded costs of £235,000. The NUR had turned the table on the BR board. This was one of the first times in which a major trade union had conducted a successful strike ballot under the new Tory laws and won its case in the courts. The BR board behaved like any unsuccessful wealthy client with a frivolous claim: it sacked its lawyer.

The 24-hour nationwide strike went ahead at one minute past midnight on 21 June, the day after Lord Donaldson rejected BR's appeal. Support for action was solid as the strike brought the national rail network to a standstill. Reports flooded into Unity House that nothing was moving on BR. On London Underground, where the union had conducted a successful second ballot over the Action Stations plan as well as a separate ballot over train operators' pay and guards' differentials, a 24-hour walk out began from the close of traffic. LUL management ran 'ghost trains' through closed stations to give the illusion that trains were still running. BR tried a similar publicity stunt that rapidly backfired when it invited the press to a photo opportunity of non-existent trains running between Twyford and Henley. The union's AGM, convening at Newcastle four days after the first strike, heard reports from branches around the country of the strike's progress, and of demonstrations of support from the public, never the most enthusiastic supporters of industrial action on the railways, with cafes and pubs supplying free tea and sandwiches. The second one-day stoppage on 28 June, held during the AGM, was also solid. The AGM also heard that, in a move reminiscent of the infamous Osborne judgment, two NUR members had tried unsuccessfully to obtain injunctions against their own union to halt the strike.

Several developments during the strike piled pressure on the BR board. The end of the Newcastle AGM coincided with the announcement of an award of the Rail Staffs National Tribunal (RSNT) of an 8.8 per cent increase in basic rates for BR salaried staff. The day before the third strike day on 5 July, BR announced record profits of some £200 million. Two days later RSNT recommended in favour of TSSA that salaried staff should be paid the 8.8 per cent increase with no strings attached. The successful TSSA pay claim handed the NUR a powerful propaganda tool in relation to BR's miserly 7 per cent offer. The issue of the TSSA claim helped to widen the dispute. Consultations took place at Unity House between the NUR, ASLEF, TSSA and the CS&EU to discuss coordinating action. As previously agreed through the Rail Federation, ASLEF balloted members on a ban on overtime and rest day working and its membership voted to take action from 12 July, the same day as the next scheduled NUR 24-hour stoppage. Electricians of the EETPU working alongside NUR staff in electrical control rooms and workshops also voted to take action.

The response of BR management was near panic. Personnel boss Trevor Toolan hurriedly sent a fax to the rail unions, sent at 9.25 in the evening of Monday 10 July, requesting urgent talks at ACAS as well as convening a meeting of the Rail Staff National Council on the following day. His fax, written in a frantic scrawl which was reproduced with much mirth in the union newspaper, requested a response within five minutes. The fax appeared to concede the issue of a pay claim for NUR staff which matched the RSNT's offer to TSSA staff of 8.8 per cent though there was no indication of concessions on the abandonment of national collective bargaining. The ACAS talks got underway the next day but were quickly halted when it became clear that BR was attempting to claw back on the 8.8 per cent offer by imposing strings. The fourth 24-hour strike, with ASLEF joining in, went ahead two days later. The resolve of management was crumbling. The BR board dropped the conditions it had previously attached to the pay claim. The executives of TSSA and ASLEF then decided to accept the 8.8

per cent award, but the NUR executive held out, sensing that it could win further concessions on the pay award and not wanting to give up on the issue of national pay bargaining machinery. The fifth day of action went ahead as planned the following week. The strike remained solid and shut down the system completely. When BR rejected further negotiations on the day after the fifth strike they were immediately told that the union would stage another strike the following week. The continual weekly hammer blows of the weekly July stoppages proved too much for management. By the time of the sixth strike BR was forced to concede that it would be willing to go to ACAS over the issue of retaining national collective bargaining. The union's executive, consulting its branches, decided to accept the 8.8 per cent pay offer, with no strings attached, and to enter into ACAS negotiations on the issue of bargaining machinery. On 27 July, the day after the sixth 24-hour strike, further action was suspended.

The acceptance of the pay offer and the suspension of the strikes did not signal an end to the union's concerns about low pay, but the strikes had wrung a great climb down from the BR board. In its aftermath Ken Toolan was eased out as personnel boss and BR moderated some of its more extreme stances. LUL management also backed away from further confrontation. The simultaneous strikes on London Underground over the issue of Action Stations forced LUL management to abandon its much hated scheme for advanced promotion for 'blue eyed boys'. The events of the summer of 1989 on the railways signalled something more profound than the immediate issues which gave rise to the strikes. Through clever use of the tactic of weekly one-day strikes, the effective use of propaganda and publicity and, above all, through the solidarity of its members, the union had won a significant victory over an obstinate BR management. The strikes of 1989 did not achieve all the union's aims. Nor did they usher in a new golden age for the railways. Far from it. The privatisation of the network, presaged in policy pronouncements by the Tories for some time, loomed large on the horizon. The eventual model for privatisation, the chopping up of BR into a chaotic multitude of companies, may have been suggested by the more extreme elements of the Conservative Party as a way of attacking the power of the national railway unions in the aftermath of the summer of strikes. This was to be one of the privately admitted but publicly unstated aims of the eventual break-up of BR. In this respect even greater challenges lay ahead. But what the 1989 strikes did do was to demonstrate that collective action and solidarity were not a thing of the past. The demoralisation that had followed the miners' defeat within the union was well and truly over.

# 5
# A Train Called Freedom

THE BITTER LABOUR STRUGGLES OF the 1980s took place against a wider international background of intensifying confrontation between the superpowers and the final act of the 50-year global standoff between the Soviet Union and the United States known as the Cold War. On the ground, the election of right wing governments such as that of Margaret Thatcher in Britain and Ronald Reagan in the United States had led to onslaughts against the trade union movements in both countries, the breaking up of the welfare state and massive increases in military spending. Abroad Reagan and Thatcher launched a new worldwide campaign against the evils of communism.

There was much to condemn in the 'actually existing socialism' of the Soviet bloc – controlled as it was by one party states which denied basic civil liberties such as freedom of speech, the right of unions to independently organise and the right to strike – rights which trade unionists in Britain were fighting to defend. But to the neo-conservative governments of the 1980s the new Cold War was more than a campaign for the civil liberties of those behind the iron curtain. Anti-communism to Thatcher and Reagan meant succour and support in the form of military and political aid to corrupt regimes and military dictatorships around the world.

Nowhere was the last chapter of the Cold War more viciously played out than in South Africa, where in the 1980s the apartheid state went through its last death throes amidst a rising tide of popular unrest and industrial action, led by the outlawed African National Congress (ANC). Across the whole of southern Africa the USSR and USA, backed by the UK, fought a bloody proxy war across the so-called frontline states. In the name of anti-communism Thatcher and Reagan gave tacit support to apartheid, refusing to implement an international boycott of trade and sporting links while condemning the activities of the ANC as terrorism. The South African liberation movement was supported in Britain by a growing band of campaign groups, community and religious organisations and trade unions that helped to build up a popular campaign against the apartheid state. Within South Africa trade unionism played a crucial role in the overthrow of apartheid. The whole racist edifice of the South African state was built on the exploitation of human labour. In the midst of the industrial defeats of the mid 1980s in the aftermath of the failure of the miners' strike, the life and death struggles of trade unionists in South Africa came to symbolise an unbending spirit of resistance.

Transport by ship and rail were crucial to the colonisation of South Africa and the apartheid state that arose from it. The discovery of gold in the Transvaal in 1886 began the process of urbanisation and industrialisation of the South African economy. Shipping and railway companies had knitted together the vast colonial interests of the region facilitating the movement of gold, coal, copper and bauxite from mines as well as the workers who toiled in them. Locomotive engines, carriages and rails made in Britain were shipped to South Africa on ships flying the red ensign of the British merchant marine. As British colonial interests increased their control over the region, a dense network of railways spread its tentacles out into the African hinterland and British flagged merchant ships carried the wealth of South Africa to the coffers of the City of London. As South Africa industrialised in the 1920s and 1930s the railways were used to transport African workers to the cities. The vast network of railways provided the very sinews of the apartheid system. The exploitation of labour relied on the mass movement of workers from tribal homelands to the townships and new urban centres. After the establishment of the apartheid state in 1948 this system became formalised with the establishment of the notorious Pass Laws, which forbade Africans from settling in the cities and led to the establishment of the so-called native Bantustans. At its height some 80 per cent of freight moved by rail in South Africa, and tens of millions of workers whose labour kept the apartheid system going, travelled by rail. The South African railways were nationalised, along with the country's dock facilities, as early as 1910, when the South African Railways and Harbours Administration (SARHA) was created. Later SARHA became the South African Transport Services (SATS) and came to control the country's national air carrier. SATS became one of South Africa's largest employers. When SATS workers confronted their employers they were thus facing not merely a private company but were challenging directly the apartheid state.

Railway trade unionism was a strange creature in apartheid South Africa. From the late nineteenth century white workers had organised themselves into whites only trade unions which looked to the European – and particularly the British – trade union movement for inspiration. Under legislation passed in the 1920s African workers were expressly barred from membership of many craft and industrial unions. Some unions, such as the National Union of Railway and Harbour Servants of South Africa (NURHAS), founded in 1915 and directly modelled on the British NUR, were officially non racial but controlled by white workers who monopolised all the most skilled jobs. During the 1920s NURHAS was virtually taken over by a branch of the infamous Broederbond, the Afrikaner secret society that later came to dominate the apartheid state. A whites only union known as Die Spoorbond was created and worked hand in glove with SARHA to create a workforce dominated by whites. Under the so-called 'Civilised Labour' policy, initiated by the Afrikaner dominated Pact government of the 1920s, white workers on the South African state railways were guaranteed benefits such as union representation, free training, lifetime job security and pensions. Black South Africans, by contrast, were treated as temporary contract labourers, excluded from all but the most menial and dangerous jobs, forbidden union representation and the right to strike. Black and so-called 'coloured' railway and harbour workers were housed in cramped single sex compounds, near to docks and rail depots. On the Cape Town docks, where militancy among dockers gave an early impetus to the creation of a national non-racial union, workers were housed in a disused gaol on the harbour's breakwater. Most black railway workers in the early twentieth century were illiterate migrant labourers working often hundreds of miles away from their tribal homelands.

Organising trade unions in such conditions was difficult in the extreme. Transport workers were amongst the first Africans to take industrial action and to try to form unions. The first major known example of industrial action by African workers took place on the Durban docks in 1895 when 200 dockers went on strike for higher pay. Before and after the First World War there were major strikes in the mining industry and in 1919 the Industrial and Commercial Workers Union (ICWU), the first nationally based union for African workers, was founded in Cape Town. The ICWU was particularly active in the major port cities, staging a successful strike by 2,000 dockers at Cape Town in December 1919. The ICWU peaked at 100,000 members but collapsed towards the end of the 1920s amid internal factionalism. Other attempts at mobilising among African workers such as the Federation of Non-European Trade Unions (FNETU) were severely hampered by the hostility of the state and employers as well as by splits within the small but influential Communist Party of South Africa about the role of trade unions and the nature of class struggle in a multi-racial society. The worldwide depression of the late 1920s hit black workers particularly hard, undefended as they were by strong collective bargaining structures. As a result wages paid to black SARHA workers were cut back by up to 20 per cent between 1929 and 1931. With the return of prosperity in the mid 1930s profits from the docks and railways soared. Major ports such as Cape Town were booming as the mineral wealth of South Africa, drawn by freight trains from the country's industrial heartlands, was exported to Europe. But the wage cuts imposed during the depression and the miserable working conditions for African workers stayed in place. Black workers remained insecure contract employees, without any rights of union representation, housed in cramped and unsanitary hostels under the draconian authority of SARHA.

The South African Railway and Harbour Workers Union (SARHWU) was formed in Cape Town in March 1936. It drew its initial strength from the highly politicised dock workers in the port, but soon grew to embrace workers from the city's Salt River railway works and from towns such as Braamfontein and Durban, and within six months had a membership of over 1,300. Without official recognition the only way that the union could organise was by collecting subs by hand and a lack of funds hindered the union from organising from the start. Early organising support was given by individual members of the South African Communist Party, which had recently dropped its policy of opposition to organising African workers. A slow but persistent effort at organising built the union up. The new union soon affiliated with the South African Council of Trade Unions (SACTU), which was aligned to the African National Congress and sought to promote the formation of non-racial unions as part of a wider political and economic struggle for social justice in South Africa. A key aim of the strategy of the union during this early period can be summarised in the slogan 'one industry, one union', whereby all workers in an industry, black or white, were to have an equal voice in one organisation. It was a statement of industrial and racial solidarity which drew from the same well of beliefs that had motivated the trade unionists in the early years of the twentieth century when all industry unions such as the NUR were created.

During the war years the union succeeded in building up limited gains. The black trade unions adopted a policy of collaborating with employers and the state during the war against fascism and, in turn, conditions for transport workers slowly improved. These gains were entirely lost in the post-war years, and with the election of the National Party and the formal creation of apartheid in 1948. Political and industrial organising was forced underground as virtually all progressive organisations, including trade unions, were banned and their officers interned. So began the darkest and most heroic chapter in the history of the anti-apartheid struggle: the long, bleak period of the 1950s and 1960s when the state almost succeeded in crushing the liberation movement. During this period, the time of the infamous treason trials (including the trial and imprisonment of Nelson Mandela, Walter Sisulu, Oliver Tambo and other leaders of the ANC), virtually all trade union activity was banned. SARHWU was effectively wound up as a functioning trade union, its leading officers thrown in prison. It managed to function only as a clandestine organisation, with a few of its activists being drawn into Umkhonto we Sizwe (MK), or Spear of the Nation, the underground armed wing of the liberation movement. Lawrence Ndzanga, the first national president of SARHWU, was detained in 1969 along with his wife Rita and several others. Ndzanga later died in detention. In 1976 railwayman and SARHWU organiser Harry Gwala, who had already served an eight year sentence for political activities, was arrested with nine others for attempting to revive SACTU, the first non-racial union federation in South African history. He and his comrades were tortured, using methods which included electric shocks, before being sentenced to life imprisonment. While in prison his wife died and Harry Gwala developed motor neurone disease.

But the apparent victory of the apartheid system was short lived. The economic growth of the 1960s and 1970s brought more black South Africans into urban industrial jobs. The huge disparities which developed between the massive profits being made by the great corporations which dominated the South African economy and the low wages and terrible conditions of the mass of the country's workforce led to increasing industrial unrest in the 1970s. Spontaneous walk outs by dockers, bus drivers and other transport workers initiated a wave of rolling strikes that began in Durban in 1973 and spread to mining, textile and metal working industries. A new era of trade union activism began, encouraged by the existing underground network but infused with a younger generation of activists. The new unionism of the 1970s sought to make links between the industrial struggle and the aims and objectives of political movements within civil society. Employers and the state responded to the new activism with a mixture of repression and conciliation. While the initial strikes were violently suppressed, new legislation was brought in which created an elaborate industrial relations machinery of works councils and liaison committees. In practice these new mechanisms were a sham, designed to give the appearance of compromise while retaining the whip hand for the employer.

The new industrial activism of the 1970s coincided with mass action by school students against the imposition of Afrikaans language teaching and the resulting demonstrations and stay away strikes known as the Soweto uprising drew on the support of the new generation of trade unionists. The Soweto uprising culminated in 1976 with massive state repression and the shooting of over 500 people, including many school children, and marked a turning point in the downfall of the apartheid system. The apartheid state began to make apparently significant concessions to African workers, including granting the right to specifically registered unions to formally collect union subs as well as negotiate legally binding wage deals, and in very limited circumstances, take industrial action. The aim of these concessions was to split the industrial wing from the political wing of the liberation movement by persuading trade unions to partially recognise the apartheid state by formally registering under the new machinery. The new state policies at first split the trade union movement, with some organisations signing up to the new mechanisms. At the same time SATS fostered the creation of a black staff association, known as BLATU, effectively run by management, as a check on militancy. Attempts to form a united trade union movement linked to the anti-apartheid struggle were stymied by the differences between different types of union. In the late 1970s there emerged a plethora of community-based general unions, which were regionally organised with few specific links to particular industries. These unions were largely political organisations, created from outside the workplace, and tended to be structurally weak with fluctuating memberships. Transport workers were represented by at least three different community-based general unions, the SAAWHU, the GAWU and the MGWUSA. It soon became apparent that what was needed was wholesale rejuvenation of industrial trade unionism linked to the political struggle. With the creation of the United Democratic Front (UDF) in 1984 churches and community groups were given a powerful focus for collective action. Attempts at creating a united industrial front bore fruit in 1985 with the creation of COSATU and the revival of SARHWU, which was re-launched in October 1986 as a result of the amalgamation of transport workers sections of the main general union. A powerful united front of transport workers on the railways, docks and airports had been created which was to confront one of the most important sectors of the South African economy, a vital linchpin in the apartheid system.

SARHWU's revival came at a critical moment in the unravelling of the apartheid state. For four months the whole country had been under a state of emergency, imposed by President P.W. Botha on 12 June 1986 in response to a mounting wave of unrest arising out of the tenth anniversary of the Soweto uprising of 1976. Abroad, international popular disgust at the apartheid system and at the continuing imprisonment of the leading figures of the liberation movement, especially Nelson Mandela, at the notorious Robben Island prison, was placing increasing demands on Western governments and international bodies such as the United Nations and the Commonwealth to put pressure on the Botha regime to dismantle the apartheid state. Within days of the state of emergency being declared the ANC President Oliver Tambo called for nationwide 'stay aways' which eventually were to involve some 86 million people. Under the rules of the state of emergency all forms of industrial action were declared illegal. Over 3,000 activists were detained, including over 900 trade union leaders, officials and shop stewards.

SARHWU sought to link the basic grievances of transport workers to the wider struggle of the liberation movement. Working conditions on the South African railways in the 1980s were little improved since the first foundation of SARHWU. Most black railway workers were on basic seasonal labouring contracts and were housed in crowded, unhygienic, all male hostels located at great distances from their homes and families. Monthly deductions were made to pay for the provision of a diet of poor quality maize 'mealie-meal' porridge. Wages were low with basic earnings for depot staff beginning at R136 per month. Workers were subject to a system of petty fines and deductions for lateness, instant dismissal and arrest – all administered through a system of disciplinary courts and enforced by the hated South African railway police, who, armed with shamboks and assault rifles, oversaw the black workforce like an army of occupation. The revived SARHWU sought to mobilise workers against conditions in the compounds. Clandestine meetings were held in the canteens and beer halls. Elected hostel committees were formed to draw up lists of grievances to present to management. At the giant Delmore hostel near the Germiston depot outside of Cape Town, where 7,000 workers were housed in a cramped single sex compound, a protest against the poor quality mealie meal led to a full blown food boycott. News of the action spread to further hostels as other workers refused to eat in the SATS canteens. The boycott succeeded in recruiting thousands of new members to SARHWU.

It was against this background that members of the NUR decided to take solidarity action. Up to the mid 1980s support for the anti-apartheid struggle by British trade unionists had been well intentioned but largely token. Resolutions against apartheid were passed at virtually every AGM of the NUR throughout the 1970s and early 1980s and these resulted in NUR delegates voting on similar motions at the TUC annual conference. In addition the union gave around £100 annually to the British Anti-Apartheid Movement. This minimal support reflected the relatively low level of international activity by the British trade union movement as a whole; the unions paid lip service to a variety of international causes including South Africa but did little to build real bonds of solidarity between workers beyond yearly junkets by official delegations to various communist and non-communist countries. The TUC kept organisations such as SACTU at arm's length because it was not a member of the pro-western International Confederation of Free Trade Unions but, rather, was a member of the Soviet-aligned World Federation of Trade Unions. As the struggle in South Africa reached its height, with the calling of the state of emergency, there was increasing dissatisfaction with this situation. SACTU had established a London headquarters and it encouraged South African unions to pair up with their British equivalents. The visit to London of Mike Roussos, SARHWU's education officer and a member of the newly founded United Democratic Front, in the spring of 1986 on a fundraising mission drew attention to the paucity of action and prompted a group of NUR activists in the London region to found Rail Against Apartheid (RAA). Launched on 23 April 1986 at a mass meeting open to all members at Friends House in the Euston Road, RAA was from the beginning designed to be a solidarity campaign with a difference. Rather than working through the bureaucratic structures of the union the idea behind RAA was to build solidarity from the bottom up by taking the anti-apartheid message directly into the workplace. In the words of NUR signalman and executive member Geoff Revell, one of the campaign's original founders, RAA 'just wanted to get on with it' by a series of step by step initiatives designed to raise consciousness and build solidarity at the workplace and in all the forums of the union. Doreen Weppler, a guard at Liverpool Street, was elected secretary and Revell was chosen as chairman. Starting off in a small way by raising money for a banner, RAA commissioned an art teacher and pupils at a comprehensive school at Gravesend, Kent to design and make the banner. From the very start it was agreed that all money should be raised from rank and file activities rather than from central union funds. General Secretary Jimmy Knapp gave support by enabling RAA to set up a bank account and within days the first £100 was raised. Further money was raised through the sale of solidarity badges designed by Revell and Weppler showing a striking logo of black and white hands clasped in solidarity. The badges were designed to provoke debate and discussion in the workplace. The campaign snowballed with Geoff Revell and Doreen Weppler travelling the country addressing meetings to try and bring together all members who wanted to put energy into solidarity work around the initiatives of RAA. All who became involved wanted their union to play a leadership role in solidarity with the struggle in South Africa. RAA organised a fringe meeting at the union's July AGM at Weston-Super-Mare addressed by COSATU's publicity officer Mike Pertz, the room so packed that the doors had to be shut to comply with fire regulations. As well as playing their part in the larger campaigns and demonstrations RAA activists staged protests in many parts of the country. One such example was the pickets against the use of the NUR organised Great Western Hotel, Paddington by Lion Worldwide Travel, a cover organisation for the pro-apartheid Friends of Springbok. This protest forced a promise from the hotel management that it would no longer accept bookings from Lion Worldwide Travel. NUR reps at BREL Derby threatened to organise a walk out if a visiting group of South African rail bosses entered the place of work. There were many other such protests which all conveyed the same message: 'if you go near NUR members' workplaces expect problems'. Money for campaigns and direct aid to what was now regarded by NUR members as its sister union was raised. Some £3,000 was raised on one CND anti-cruise missile march in central London. Because of the sensitive issue of direct links regular meetings were held with SACTU officials in their London offices in Mark Street and through them RAA was kept in contact with SARHWU officials at the Johannesburg offices at COSATU House.

The news out of South Africa was dramatic. In February 1987, just before they were due to travel to London to speak at a series of RAA organised meetings, the new General Secretary of SARHWU, Ntai Sello, and union organiser Paul Mabuso were arrested along with four other SARHWU leaders for their role in organising the food boycotts. All six were sentenced under the new state of emergency at a state tribunal to four months detention. If SATS' management thought that by arresting the leadership opposition would be crushed they were seriously mistaken. On 12 March 1987 a driver at a South African Transport Services City Deep container depot in Johannesburg, Andrew Nedzamba, was sacked for handing over R401 in cash on delivery receipts (the equivalent of about £5) two days late. From this minor infringement of management rules began the longest strike in the 52-year history of the South African railways. Within 24 hours

I attended the 1997 AGM at Dundee as a youth delegate. During that meeting I picked up a Rail Against Apartheid leaflet. I realised that there was a big rank and file campaign on the go. I had always been personally against racism and against apartheid but apart from supporting the anti-apartheid movement I had never come across anything that I could get involved with in a big way. With this being my own union which seemed to be doing something different, with direct links to the South African union, it really captured my imagination and I felt it was important that everybody pitched in. It was something that was really close to home. It hit a chord. The campaign focused on workers doing the exact same job as you and your colleagues, but the circumstances in which they had to live were so brutally different you couldn't help but get involved. For a lot of workers in the NUR who ended up supporting the campaign it was that that hit them first and foremost. These were guards on the train, platform workers or cleaners who were brutalised by the whole regime for doing the same job as we did. That hit you between the eyes. It wasn't just solidarity between head offices of the unions, it involved direct participation for the rank and file.

Alan Pottage

several hundred of his fellow workers walked out in solidarity with him. A local protest against victimisation led to a wider confrontation with SATS and the state. A heavily policed mass meeting of 4,000 railway workers at COSATU House demanded Nedzamba's immediate reinstatement but also called for recognition of SARHWU by SATS. The strike spread to other depots in the Transvaal and by the beginning of April 20,000 men were on strike.

The prospect of the national whites-only election, due to be held in early May, heightened the state of tension surrounding the strike. As the momentum of the strike gathered pace the apartheid state became increasingly alarmed, using police and troops to guard railway property and intimidate strikers. The union's offices and COSATU House in Cape Town, which became the strike's headquarters, were regularly raided. SATS management refused to talk to SARHWU, claiming that strike action was down to 'a communist plot' and that its workforce was already represented by the staff association BLATU, which worked with management to organise scabbing resulting in violent confrontations. Railway carriages parked in sidings were set ablaze and sections of track were dismantled by SARHWU permanent way workers. A deadline for a return to work set by SATS for 21 April came and went with no sign of a faltering in support for the strike. Despite the threat of mass sackings, between 16,000 and 20,000 men remained on strike. On 22 April, as armed police and government security forces stood by, a train carrying SARHWU members was attacked by a large group of BLATU members as it pulled into Germiston Station. Tear gas canisters were thrown into the carriages carrying the strikers and for the next two hours a pitched battle ensued in which at least three strikers and BLATU members were killed and many dozens wounded. The situation became even more serious at Doornfontein when police opened fire on a group of SARHWU strikers on their way to Germiston, killing three. One week later, in a clear example of how violence begets violence, the bodies of four badly beaten and burnt strike breakers were found in rough ground at Prolecon, outside Cape Town. Heavily armed police, backed up by helicopters and armoured cars, raided COSATU House, destroying property and arresting between 300 and 400 strikers who were detained under state of emergency legislation, including the union's President, Justice Langa and the Transvaal Regional Secretary, Johannes Ngcobo, both of whom were due to travel to Britain at the invitation of RAA.

The arrest of most of SARHWU's leading officers prompted RAA to drastic action. It was decided that RAA's Chair and Secretary, Geoff Revell and Doreen Weppler, should travel to South Africa to deliver the money raised by the RAA solidarity campaign directly to SARHWU at COSATU House. It was to be a fact finding trip with the object of preparing a report that would enable the union to publicise SARHWU's situation to the wider trade union movement in Britain. Because of the situation in South Africa a cover story was provided with outside help. They flew to Durban and reported to the SARHWU office there before travelling on the night train to Johannesburg. While the pair were en route to South Africa, COSATU House was devastated by two massive explosions caused by bombs placed by government agents. The union's entire membership records, all its files and equipment were lost in the explosions and subsequent ransacking by the police in the aftermath of the blasts. SARHWU was a union without a headquarters, its senior leadership in prison, its acting leadership on the run. Mike Roussos, SARHWU's education officer who was due to travel to London, was picked up the next day for alleged complicity in the Prolecon killings. Weppler and Revell, who had only learned about the bombings through the newspapers after they arrived at Johannesburg rail station, made contact with a detainees support group by chance located up the street from the destroyed COSATU House. They were taken to meet COSATU General Secretary Jai Naidoo who passed them on to the acting leadership. They then made contact with Derek Hanekom, a UDF official (now Deputy Minister for Science and Technology in the ANC led government), who was assisting what was left of the SARHWU leadership in their tireless efforts to hold the organisation together. The significant sum of money raised from the NUR membership's campaigns was extremely welcome, as was the display of solidarity in sending representatives to meet with SARHWU. The cash, now badly needed for bail money and legal fees, was drawn out on credit cards at different Johannesburg banks and delivered to SARHWU. In addition to this Weppler and Revell set out on a fact finding tour, meeting with SARHWU and COSATU colleagues and others concerned about the plight of the detained rail workers. When Hanekom asked what the union would be allowed to spend the money on he seemed extremely pleased when Doreen Weppler replied that 'the money is now SARHWU's, it is for you to decide'. After joining SARHWU as full members in a makeshift recruiting room over a shebeen in downtown Johannesburg the pair carried out the fact finding exercise. They were invited to attend as 'international observers' a meeting between SARHWU and bishops from each of the South African churches with the aim of getting the church leaders to act as intermediaries. While waiting to board a van to take them to the meeting the pair were suddenly told to leave quickly and then return. Apparently South African police interest had been aroused by the sight of a white woman and a white man in the company of black men in that area. Geoff Revell recounts how, as he and Doreen lay flat on the floor of the van, a fellow trade unionist, on learning that they were from Britain, asked them if they knew Arthur Scargill. Towards the end of their visit they gave an interview with the main anti-apartheid newspaper, the radical *New Nation*. They were informed after the interview that the security services had learned of their presence in the country and the reasons for their visit and were advised to leave South Africa as soon as possible. They returned to London where they prepared a report of the trip. The trip was crucial in building bonds of solidarity between SARHWU and the NUR, bonds that were to extend well beyond the strike. The day after Weppler and Revell left, the front page of the *New Nation* carried their picture and a report on the visit under the headline 'SARHWU You are not alone'. The NUR membership became even more determined to rally to those words.

The solidarity shown by the hundreds of RAA active supporters in part helped the strikers to hold out after the bombing of COSATU House and the imprisonment of most of the SARHWU leadership. Pressure was building on SATS to settle the strike as it extended into its third month. The railway network started to deteriorate as little maintenance work was carried out. Behind the scenes negotiations between SATS and legal representatives of SARHWU took place. Lawyers for SARHWU took SATS to court, challenging the 21 April sackings. Before the case was due to be heard a settlement was reached, promising reinstatement of the sacked strikers, an improvement to conditions in the railway hostels, permanent contracts for those with two years service and the right to elect representatives. But despite these apparent gains the union emerged from the strike in a very difficult position. Many of the leadership were still in detention under state of emergency laws. There was much victimisation of activists, many of whom were demoted or moved. In some instances members of local strike committees were re-arrested after the strike. Ntai Sello, who was detained without charge for four months, underwent psychiatric treatment after his release. Mike Roussos was imprisoned for two and a half months and was on release suffering from the effects of ill treatment. The four men found guilty of the Prolecon killings were sentenced to death. The mainstream anti-apartheid activists in the British labour movement demanded that the death sentences be commuted. RAA, in solidarity with the demands coming from SARHWU, campaigned for the release of the jailed men. 'Free the SARHWU four' became the main RAA campaign, although it was difficult to get the policy accepted on platforms provided by the mainstream labour movement. One trade union official, now a New Labour minister, displayed a shocking ignorance of the realities of industrial strife in apartheid South Africa by asking if RAA would condone striking rail workers in Britain setting fire to members of the non-striking TSSA. The SARHWU four did eventually have their sentences commuted and were released at the end of apartheid. But after the strike SATS made no moves towards official recognition of SARHWU, despite the fact that the union now had 25,000 members and was one of the country's fastest growing unions, viewed as the voice of South African transport workers around the world.

The victory of the 1987 strike was thus short lived. Though in the aftermath of the strike the union almost doubled in size, it lacked internal cohesion and became riven by regional factionalism and damaging leadership splits. Disunity made the task of recruiting new members in order to gain recognition from SATS more difficult. Despite having some 40,000 members by 1988 the union did not have a majority of the SATS African workforce which management still falsely claimed were represented by BLATU. Yet the union needed to demonstrate its ability to make substantial material gains in order to win over new members and gain recognition. This was against a background of government plans to split up and eventually privatise SATS by creating a new controlling body, Transnet, and four separate commercial arms. In the run up to privatisation the management structure of Transnet was decentralised and local managers began imposing a wage freeze and layoffs. As in Britain the writing was on the wall but lack of a coherent strategy of opposition dogged efforts to halt privatisation. A poorly coordinated 'living wage campaign', which was launched in 1988 at the height of the union's internal civil war, led to short lived and largely unsuccessful regional strikes which resulted in victimisation and over 400 redundancies. Management made some small concessions in the wake of the strikes. SATS agreed a local recognition agreement with SARHWU in Natal and new legislation seemed to lay the framework for collective bargaining, though the Act, which set up labour councils made up of representatives of all unions, perpetuated the privileged role of BLATU and also made strikes by SATS employees illegal.

In London RAA kept up a round of sustained campaigning, raising money for the organisation, calling for the release of all detainees and political prisoners. RAA became part of the international campaign to free Harry Gwala whose medical condition had deteriorated in prison. In July 1987 SACTU General Secretary John Nkadimeg spoke at the Dundee AGM on the outcome of the three month SARHWU strike, telling the meeting of the poor health of Ntai Sello and Mike Roussos after their detention. In August that year RAA helped to organise the first national convention for sanctions at Central Hall Westminster which brought together representatives of 2 million British trade unionists, plus 23 regional bodies, student groups, local anti-apartheid groups, and churches. After their release from detention Ntai Sello and Justice Langa paid a visit to Britain at the invitation of the NUR. By this stage Geoff Revell was no longer an EC member and returned to full-time work as a London Underground signalman, though a sympathetic supervisor at his workplace gave him ample time for campaigning. Revell and Doreen Weppler spoke to groups up and down the country about their experience of the visit and conditions during the 1987 strike. NUR General Secretary Jimmy Knapp lent his support to the RAA's campaign for the release of Harry Gwala, personally handing in a petition calling for his immediate release to South Africa House, signed by 30,000 trade unionists. The agitation and adverse publicity paid off as Harry Gwala was freed on medical grounds from Robben Island in November of 1988. During this period SARHWU's finances were in a parlous state; official recognition subs still had to be collected individually and this meant that the union had great difficulty merely paying its wages bill. The RAA campaign, plus direct grants from the national executive of the union, helped to keep SARHWU alive during this intense period of struggle.

Throughout 1989 SARHWU sought recognition from SATS. Against the wishes of many of its members SARHWU entered into negotiations with SATS and indicated that it would comply with management's demand that it register under the Industrial Relations Act, a much loathed piece of apartheid legislation under which unions like BLATU operated. Attempts by SARHWU to discuss the issue of wages and the future of transport workers prior to privatisation failed when SATS management refused to talk to the union until it had formally registered. Amid a rising tide of rank and file discontent with the failure of talks to make any headway, strike action seemed the only way forward for the union to maintain the support of its increasingly radicalised membership. A strike began on 1 November 1989 with a mass walk out of 800 workers at Kaserne Depot in the Southern Transvaal over a sacking which quickly spread to other parts of the country. The lack of coordination of previous strikes was overcome; some 40,000 transport workers quickly joined the strike bringing all the major railway depots, ports and harbours to a standstill. SARHWU seized the opportunity and demanded recognition by SATS, the immediate reinstatement of the 400 workers sacked after the 1988 strike in East London, changes to a new disciplinary code which outlawed strikes, a minimum wage of R1,500 (approx. £350) per month and the reinstatement by September of 1,000 workers sacked under new disciplinary code brought in by management. Attempts to negotiate an early end to the strike by SARHWU with the assistance of COSATU ended in deadlock, and SATS began mass sackings of strikers.

The strike was marked by violence on all sides as non-striking BLATU members and the transport police confronted newly armed and radicalised SARHWU members. In Durban and elsewhere SARHWU strikers, with the assistance of MK, sabotaged trains and signalling equipment, destroyed many hundreds of thousands of Rands worth of equipment. The tension of the strike was heightened by larger political events. The ANC was conducting direct though still secret talks with the apartheid state about the release of political prisoners and its eventual unbanning. Through COSATU the ANC put pressure on SARHWU not to let the strike degenerate into greater violence. There were many who suspected that state sponsored 'third force' militias, designed to wreck the prospects of a peaceful transition to majority rule, had played a clandestine role in the conflict by seeking to exacerbate the violence. Some of the worst killings took place at Germiston Station, the scene of violence in the 1987 strike. On 9 January 1990 several trainloads of SARHWU reps and members were attacked by a crowd of 1,000 BLATU vigilantes wielding clubs, machetes and knives, as SATS transport police and army looked on. The police fired tear gas onto the train forcing the SARHWU members off. Nine men were killed and there were more than a hundred serious injuries, including commuters who had been travelling without tickets. The 'Germiston Massacre' made international headlines and focused worldwide attention on the plight of South African railway workers. It later came out that SATS officials had deliberately transported the BLATU members to Germiston. In the course of the 13-week strike there were more than 50 deaths and several hundred injuries.

In the midst of this increasingly desperate situation RAA sent members back to South Africa on another fact-finding mission and to better publicise the plight of SARHWU members. The media in the outside world was portraying the killing of the striking railway workers as 'black on black' violence, ignoring the perfidious role played by SATS and the security forces who were mobilising the attacks. The General Secretary of COSATU, Jay Naidoo, approached RAA asking that it send representatives in order to monitor the progress of the strike. Geoff Revell and Alan Pottage, a young ticket office booking supervisor at Edinburgh Waverley and local rep and RAA activist, quickly arranged to fly to Johannesburg almost a week after the Germiston killings. Though they both knew that the RAA funding for the trip would eventually be raised, Revell applied for a bank loan on the premise of buying a car in order to pay quickly for the flight. SACTU used the men as couriers to take important documents to the SACTU offices in Lusaka, Zambia, before they flew on to Johannesburg. The two took the precaution of making an arrangement to phone the NUR head office in London if one or the other encountered any difficulty. This was a wise move as Geoff Revell was immediately stopped by security staff at Jan Smuts airport, and after having his passport, money and tickets taken from him was subjected to a 72-hour detention. Alan, who was behind Geoff in the queue, passed through passport control and quickly got away. Geoff was subjected to, by South African standards, a mild interrogation about the purpose of his visit before being told that he was named on a list of people who were not welcome in South Africa and that he would be held until his file 'arrived from Pretoria'. A poorly supervised trip to a toilet allowed him to reverse charges on a wall pay phone and tell the NUR in London of his plight.

After several urgent phone calls and pressure from British MPs, a reluctant British envoy agreed to intervene, calling the detention 'an own goal'. This alluded to the imminent arrival through the same airport of the sanctions busting English cricket team led by Mike Gatting. When Gatting's rebel tour arrived a bloody street battle erupted outside the airport with some demonstrators against the visit holding placards which read 'Cricketers out! Railworkers in!' Word had by now got back to London where RAA activists, including tutors and students from the union's school at Frant Place, travelled to the South African Embassy to join other protestors. One young tutor and later RMT General Secretary, Bob Crow, gained access to the embassy and staged a sit down strike before being evicted. A minor diplomatic incident seemed to be brewing. Revell was formally seen by South African authorities at the airport and informed that he was to be expelled forthwith. Served with an expulsion order mysteriously dated six months earlier, Geoff was put on the next flight to Lusaka. There he made contact with ANC officials and was taken to an ANC run military compound, then on red alert due to possible military attack by South African security forces.

Meanwhile Alan Pottage joined the SARHWU leaders who co-opted him on to their negotiating team as an international observer. Pottage was ordered back to the airport and was served with an expulsion order but persuaded immigration officials to allow him to stay in South Africa for a further seven days. He attended negotiations between SARHWU and SATS officials under the aegis of the Independent Mediation Services of South Africa. The talks were taking place just as behind the scenes discussions on the release of Nelson Mandela were under way. After marathon talks lasting four days breakthrough came on 26 January 1990. After a week Alan Pottage left to rejoin Geoff Revell in Lusaka taking with him smuggled affidavits from SARHWU recounting security force complicity in the Germiston massacre.

The SARHWU leadership so prioritised the solidarity between RAA and SARHWU that they asked me to join the negotiating team. They were telling us that had it not been for RAA's help coming at a time when COSATU House was bombed and their leadership imprisoned and tortured, the union would not have survived. The NUR lit this little ember that kept them going so that they could rebuild their strength. I was 26 at the time. I was a regional negotiator but I didn't really have the experience I have now. They said they would conduct their meetings in English so I could follow what was said. There were 40 delegations from all over South Africa, including men who had travelled many days on foot. The talks turned out to be historical because a few days after we returned the union won recognition and reinstatement of the 25,000 SATS workers who were on strike and who had been ejected from their hostels, lost their pensions, had their members maimed and shot.

Alan Pottage

The RAA trip came at the turning point in the history of apartheid's final days. In early February 1990, just after Alan Pottage and Geoff Revell had returned from Lusaka, Nelson Mandela and other political prisoners were freed, and the ANC and other political parties were unbanned. Under the agreement signed in April SATS agreed to recognise SARHWU in return for registration, and an immediate reinstatement of all strikers without loss of earning or pension rights. SATS also agreed to enter into negotiations over outstanding issues such as wages. There were to be several months of intense talks and several local strikes before SATS, now renamed Transnet, agreed to a nationwide recognition deal on 1 November 1990. By then South Africa was well on the way to finally throwing off the bonds of the apartheid state. Though setbacks and compromises lay ahead, the road to freedom for South Africa had been mapped out. SARHWU's victory was part of the wider story of the fight for freedom in South Africa. Though many had died along the way a 56 year campaign of recognition was finally won.

The NUR relationship with SARHWU broke the taboo on 'direct links' and official delegations that followed included Jimmy Knapp and a RAA activist Brian Whitehead who was proud to find himself greeting the great Justice Langa in his Soweto home. RAA was wound up at the AGM held at Ayr in 1991. At its height every district council, every grade conference and NUR members in every major city in Britain had heard the message of the RAA group. Some £20,000 was donated through Dutch intermediaries every quarter and an organisation that had started out with £100 had managed to raise hundreds of thousands more in direct donations from individual NUR members. Through the RAA, SARHWU built contacts with fellow transport workers in the International Transport Federation, including workers in Australia, New Zealand, the United States, Germany, France and Sweden. For British railway workers the example of unbending defiance, despite feeling the full weight of the apartheid state, was an inspiration. SARHWU's experience of recruitment, mobilisation and self-organisation was to

---

What I think was important about the whole thing was the absolute inspiration of workers standing up against the might and power of the forces in South Africa, showing that ultimate sacrifice, never flinching, and eventually coming out after many, many decades and winning at the end of it. Workers in Britain were being inspired by the example of the South African workers taking a stand in overturning apartheid. What they did was absolutely tremendous.

Alan Pottage

provide important lessons for railway workers in Britain in the years
to come.

The struggle of the South African railway workers and the solidarity
action of their British comrades has a contemporary significance. Just
as today there were some who questioned whether trade unions should
concern themselves with events and struggles that were not immediately
linked to the bread and butter issues that affect their membership.
According to this argument trade unionists should not get involved
in political and particularly international political campaigns. Yet in
apartheid South Africa there was no such thing as a non-political
strike. Racial oppression and economic exploitation were two sides of
the same coin; lack of trade union rights was part of a larger system
of political repression. This was as important for British workers as it
was for their South African comrades. The forces that were attempting
to subjugate and divide the South African working class were the
same as those that were trying to destroy the trade union movement
in Britain.

# 6
# *Fighting Privatisation*

## Anatomy of a Merger

THE COLLAPSE OF APARTHEID SOUTH AFRICA was but one aspect of a series of climacteric social and political upheavals that rocked the world at the end of the 1980s. Beginning in the spring of 1989 the collapse of communism in Poland, East Germany, Czechoslovakia and Russia ended the 50 year Cold War and the 75 year experiment of Soviet communism. For some the demise of the Soviet Union was the final victory of Western capitalism. Did the self-evident moral and political failure of the Soviet Union also signal the death of socialism as an idea? For many on the right and for an increasingly disillusioned number of people on the left the answer appeared to be yes. For others, the fall of the Soviet Union marked a point of renewal. The ideals of socialism, stifled and corrupted by the exercise of totalitarian power, were to be re-invented from the bottom up.

To some within the trade unions and the Labour Party international events of the late 1980s seemed to confirm that free market capitalism had triumphed and that the labour movement's long-term aim of common ownership had to be irrevocably abandoned. For British trade unions the end of the 1980s marked the absolute nadir of influence. Hemmed in by Tory legislation unions seemingly had too little power to protect their members. Privatisation, the break up of large-scale enterprises and the defeats of the 1980s had led to a steady decline in union membership. The NUR had lost 62,000 members between 1979 and 1990. The NUS had lost some 7,000 members over the same period. One way to combat the decline of union strength was to merge unions across sectors. This had been the long-term aim of the NUR with regard to unions such as ASLEF and TSSA within the transport sector. In the course of the 1980s other unions, such as GMB and MSF began to amalgamate across sectors. In the aftermath of the setbacks of the Thatcher period the leadership of the NUR and the NUS began to look at the possibility of following the same route.

The origins of the merger between the NUR and the NUS reached back to the time of the disastrous P&O strike. The strike broke out against a background of a fast disappearing merchant fleet and rapidly shrinking NUS membership. In the five years before the strike the seamen's union had lost something like 30 per cent of its membership, forcing it to raise union fees, close regional offices and freeze staff wages. In December 1986 the NUS affiliated to the TUC on the basis of an official membership of 22,896, but by the time of the strike it was widely thought inside the union that actual membership had fallen well below 15,000. An informal discussion of a possible merger took place between Jimmy Knapp and Sam McCluskie at the August 1987 TUC conference, but the need for the NUS to take decisive action became imperative with the onset of the strike. The course of the strike saw the union's position degenerate. The fines imposed by the courts during the strike had provoked an immediate cash crisis while strike pay, balloting and other expenses were eating into the union's funds. At the height of the strike the union was selling off investments, selling regional offices, and cutting union posts.

Initially the NUS leadership was publicly neutral on the issue of which union the seamen should merge with. Both the NUR and the TGWU emerged as suitors. But in the run up to the strike the EC began to tilt towards the railwaymen. It was opposed by a small but significant minority, mostly members from Region 2, representing Liverpool and Humberside who had been challenging McCluskie's control of the union since before the strike, and who wanted the union to join up with the TGWU. For several years prior to this the activists from Liverpool and Cardiff had been a thorn in the leadership's side, challenging McCluskie's handling of the crisis facing the industry. These divisions led to an acrimonious series of debates at the union's bi-annual conference at Hull in May 1988. The four day meeting was dominated by the faltering course of the P&O strike, with activists laying into Sam McCluskie's handling of the dispute. On the third day conference debated the whole issue of merger and voted to hold a union-wide three month postal ballot on merger proposals with either the TGWU or the NUR by the end of the year. The NUS executive had sought to lay the groundwork for a merger with the NUR by issuing an interim official report that came down firmly on the side of a merger with the railway union.

---

One of the problems with the NUS and the shipping industry in general was that seafarers tended to think that they were unique. In some respects they were, but then you have the same cultural issue within the older NUR members about the railway. So there was this feeling that we're different to everybody else. They weren't really generally open to amalgamation. An important element of this was that the left within the NUS had for a period of 15 to 20 years on and off been trying to push for amalgamation with the TGWU because it was felt that the T&G was an ideal industrial partner for us as an industrial strategy prior to the introduction of the ban on secondary picketing. Dockers and seafarers working together would have been virtually unbeatable. The leadership were opposed to amalgamation with the T&G because it was so large a union we would have just become a small section of the T&G. The irony is we wound up in a very radical union. The RMT, particularly since Bob Crow took over, is what a trade union should be. It is a campaigning, very active union. From a trade union activist point of view I am absolutely delighted with the RMT.

Bob Rayner

---

The report, endorsed by the leadership of the two unions, sought to build up an image of a common shared history. The two unions did indeed have much in common. At crucial points in the early 1900s railway workers and seafarers had made common cause and had drawn inspiration from their mutual history of trade union organising. The original rulebook and constitution of the seamen's union drawn up in 1887 was based on the rulebook of the old ASRS – forerunner to the NUR. During the nationwide dock strikes of August 1911 railway workers at ports such as Cardiff and Liverpool refused to cross picket lines, blacked goods trains due for the ports and informed the seamen's and dockers' unions of management's attempts to bring scabs to the quayside. Moreover the success of the dockers and seafarers in the August strikes, who successfully held out for a rise in wages from six pence per hour to eight pence despite the use of troops – and at Liverpool, two navy warships – inspired railwaymen to take their own action that same month. A wave of strikes began with unofficial action by rail workers closest to the port cities caught up in the action at the docks. The first national railway strike, which led directly to the creation of the NUR little more than a year later, was thus directly inspired by the action of the seamen. Both unions were born in the heyday of syndicalist inspired belief in 'all industry unions' – the creation of powerful blocs of organised labour which would cut across sectional and craft divides and present a united front to the employers. In the case of the NUR the long-term goal of amalgamation with ASLEF and the Railway Clerks Association (the predecessor of TSSA) eluded it, though a measure of coordination was achieved by the creation of the Rail Federation in 1982. In addition to this it was pointed out that the NUR and the NUS found themselves dealing with the same set of industrial problems. Railway workers and seafarers worked side by side in ports and docks. Both unions often sat down to negotiate with the same sets of employers such as Caledonian MacBrayne and Sealink.

The three month period of postal balloting of NUS members began in September 1988 and the results were announced in April the following year. Forty-five per cent of the 16,100 NUS membership took part. The results showed decisive support for the merger with the NUR. Some 4,901 votes were cast in favour of the principle of a merger with another union, as opposed to 2,472 against. Of the two suitor unions 4,636 voted for the NUR while 3,268 voted for the TGWU. Merger talks got underway in earnest after the results of the postal vote became known. Working parties from both unions examined the constitutional and financial issues involved in a merger. A new rulebook and constitution were drafted. The new rules allowed for the creation of a council of executives which consisted of a general committee covering the ex NUR general grades and a shipping committee made up of the ex NUS shipping grades. Both committees were to deal separately with matters affecting their respective sectors but sit together as the union's Council of Executives on matters affecting the whole of the union. The issue of the name of the new union was a delicate matter, as the membership of both unions looked with pride to their respective industries and traditions. The old names of the two unions were steeped in labour history and yet were becoming anachronistic. The NUR had for many years recruited amongst bus drivers, dock workers and catering staff. In an age in which more and more women were joining the industry it was felt inappropriate to use the old titles of 'seamen' and 'railwaymen'. The new name, The National Union of Rail, Maritime and Transport Workers sought to retain the traditional associations of the two merged unions but also to signal the creation of a new specialist union for all transport workers. According to law both unions balloted their members in the summer of 1990. The results, announced at the NUR AGM in Liverpool, showed a three to one majority (25,178 to 8,700) of NUR members voting for the merger on a 30 per cent postal turnout. The NUS voted by an even greater majority of seven to one (4,229 to 644) in favour of the merger on a 25 per cent postal vote. The inaugural meeting of the executive of the new union was held at Maritime House, Clapham, the old headquarters of the NUS, on 25 September 1990.

The membership of the new union emerged from the battles of the 1980s bloodied but unbowed. Though whole swathes of the industry had been hived off to the private sector, the core of the public transport system, the national rail network, remained in public ownership. The fall of Margaret Thatcher in the autumn of 1990 might have seemed like it presaged a new kinder, gentler form of conservatism. Yet within a few months of her fall the new government of John Major embarked on one last great effort of privatisation, the break up of BR. The privatisation of BR challenged the very existence of the RMT. With limited support from the Labour Party hierarchy, the RMT launched a campaign of opposition, including strike action in defence of the nationalised industry and its members. A series of 24-hour strikes in the run up to privatisation culminated in a bitter ten-week signal workers' strike in the summer and autumn of 1994. Despite the shattering of BR into over a hundred companies the union managed to hold on to its bargaining position as representative of the largest union in the industry. But privatisation was not stopped in its tracks, and in the aftermath of the break-up of BR the union suffered an organisational crisis that resulted in a massive loss of revenue and membership.

The privatisation of the railways had been on the cards for almost a decade. In 1987, Kenneth Irvine, a former BR manager working for the Thatcherite think tank the Adam Smith Institute, drafted a proposal to break up BR into separate companies. But the idea was deemed too politically unpopular to be acted on, even by the Thatcher government. Though she had an avowed dislike of railways, Thatcher had fought shy of privatising the rail network. Her political instincts told her that railways were popular with the general public and she allegedly told the arch advocate of privatisation Nicholas Ridley: 'Rail privatisation will be the Waterloo of this government. Please never mention the railways to me again.' She later changed her mind and in November 1990 Cecil Parkinson announced to the House of Commons that the government was 'determined to privatise British Rail'. In the event it fell to Thatcher's inept successor John Major to take up the proposal when he came into office in the autumn of 1990.

A government working party, consisting of ministers and officials from the Department of Transport and the Treasury's privatisation unit, was set up in late 1990. It was this body which was responsible for the biggest fiasco associated with rail privatisation, the split between operations and infrastructure, based on Irvine's original model. Other forms of privatisation, such as the effective re-creation of the old pre-nationalised 'big four' railways based on regions, the sell-off of the three main BR passenger businesses, Network South East, Intercity and Regional Railways, and the sale of BR as a single unit, were all given short shrift. It is now clear why the Major government refused to countenance the sale of BR as a single unit. According to transport journalist Christian Wolmar:

> 'It was felt that a BR plc would preclude any competition and not have challenged the position of the strong nationally organised trade unions within the industry. Reducing the power of the trade unions was one of the hidden motives for rail privatisations, expressed privately by Tory ministers on many occasions but never boasted about in public.'

The later decision to hive-off BR's engineering and track maintenance into 13 regionally based British Rail Infrastructure companies, or Briscos, was similarly designed with the covert objective of attacking organised labour. An anonymous BR manager told Wolmar: 'this was the unspoken agenda. Ministers told us in private that they wanted to break up the unions, but of course they did not say so in public.'

None of this figured in the election manifesto published by the Tories in time for the surprise election victory of John Major in April 1992. The manifesto commitment to privatise was vague, promising a greater involvement for the private sector while stating that BR would continue to be responsible for all track infrastructure: 'our aim will be...to reflect regional and local identity...we want to...recapture the spirit of the old regional companies'. With the Labour Party widely expected to either win or at least form the largest party in a hung parliament the issue of rail privatisation was given little comment. In the event the Tories under Major formed the government with a tiny 20-seat majority and set about implementing their plans with indecent haste.

> At first we didn't know how it was going to take place. Were they going to sell the British Railways Board? Were they going to sell the London Underground to somebody for a lot of money? What we were aware of was that before us British Telecoms, electricity and the water boards had been privatised. Sections of our own members had been privatised. There was the floatation of the National Freight Corporation. The hotels had been put out and bought up. We didn't understand the complete and utter chaos it was going to bring.
>
> Geoff Revell

Proposals were published in the July 1992 white paper *New Opportunities for Railways*. This set out a programme of franchising of train operations to private companies. Other operations, such as repair and maintenance of infrastructure, the ownership and leasing of rolling stock were to be sold off. New rolling stock and infrastructure companies, the infamous Roscos and Infracos, were to be created out of the rump of BR. A new publicly owned track authority, or Railtrack, was to be created. The privatisation of this new track authority was not mentioned in the primary legislation, and was only carried out in the last gasp of the Major administration before the general election of May 1997. In the interim a protracted period of getting the legislation through parliament witnessed a concerted public campaign, which embraced the transport unions, voluntary bodies, transport experts as well as the Labour opposition, the Liberal Democrats, and even some Tory MPs. The RMT helped fund a public campaign that aimed to galvanise public sentiment against privatisation. In February 1993 a 'Save Our Railways' campaign group was launched by the RMT and gained support from other unions, alongside railway users groups, amenity societies, environmental and transport pressure groups. 'Save Our Railways' later enjoyed a minor victory in court against the government but did not stop the process. Leading Labour politicians, including Clare Short, Frank Dobson and John Prescott, spoke out against the privatisation bill with great rhetorical flourish but with little practical effect. Memorably Clare Short told the House of Commons: 'Anyone contemplating bidding for any part of the rail network should know that there will be no gravy train for fat cats out of this one and that Labour intends that the rail system should remain in public ownership.' Even the newly elected leader of the opposition Tony Blair spoke in favour of retaining BR in public ownership. Opposition within the ranks of the Tories was blunted through the death of a leading opponent of privatisation Robert Adley MP, who famously described rail privatisation as 'the poll tax on wheels', in the summer of 1993. Despite hundreds of amendments the legislation which enabled privatisation to go ahead became law in November 1993.

## Strikes Against Privatisation, 1993

The union's resistance to privatisation took place alongside parallel struggles by other workers, including miners, firefighters and workers at Ford and Timex at Dundee which seemed at the time to indicate a renewal of industrial militancy. Coordinated action against rail privatisation under the umbrella of the European TUC's campaign against unemployment seemed possible. Inter-union rivalries were once again put aside in common interests of members. In late March the RMT in coordination with ASLEF made plans for industrial action timed to coincide with the NUM's campaign against further pit closures and the privatisation of British Coal, and action by TGWU members on the London buses. The core of the action was to fight the threat of job cuts and contracting out of BR services in the drive to privatisation. The union's case for the dispute was that under an agreement signed in 1985 BR undertook a promise that, in return for railway workers agreeing to compulsory redeployment when necessary, there would be no compulsory redundancies. But the BR board, in the throes of privatisation effectively reneged on this, stating that no employer could guarantee 'jobs for life'. Members were balloted and in an overwhelming vote (26,097 to 10,314 on a 64 per cent turnout) decided to stage a 24-hour strike on Friday 2 April. BR challenged the union's mandate for the stoppage but in response to BR's call to halt the strike Jimmy Knapp retorted that: 'the message is clear, enough is enough'.

Further action was threatened unless BR could undertake to stand by the 1985 agreement on no compulsory redundancies. In retaliation for the first strike BR ended automatic check off of union dues (in use since 1965). Intensive negotiations took place on 16 April. Talks broke up after an acrimonious eight-minute meeting during which BR Chairman Sir Bob Reid was said to have been abusive to Jimmy Knapp who subsequently complained: 'I have never been treated like that in 35 years in the industry.' A second 24-hour strike went ahead on 16 April.

After the second strike the RMT began to plan further action. Even though ASLEF pulled out there were grounds for optimism that BR would come to an agreement. On 20 April Jimmy Knapp proposed talks. The RMT was 'going to test BR's good faith'. A letter from the BR Chairman Sir Bob Reid to Labour shadow transport spokesman John Prescott stated that, while unable to guarantee no future job cuts, 'the [BR] board has no plans currently for any compulsory redundancies' and that it also had 'no plans for a major extension of the use of contract labour in the area of track maintenance during the next couple of years'. The union's left leaning executive was evenly split on whether to take further action or enter into talks. After a nine hour meeting at Unity House ended in deadlock it was decided to hold a ballot, recommending a rejection of BR's proposals and further strikes. In the run up to the ballot BR issued a series of statements attacking the strikes as damaging to the industry, citing losses of £10 million per strike day. It also restated that, while it could give no absolute guarantee on job cuts, it had 'no plans' for redundancies or contracting labour for track maintenance 'over the next couple of years'. The ballot resulted in a very narrow vote (18,544 to 18,361 on a 62.5 per cent turnout) to resume talks. The hollowness of BR's 'no plans' statements were to ring in the ears of the membership in the aftermath of privatisation. At a late stage in the passage of the bill that privatised BR the government inserted an amendment of its own which gave BR new legal powers, that overturned Promotion, Transfer and Redundancy (PT&R) arrangements which guaranteed the rights of workers to progress through the industry, and be transferred from one sector of the industry to another. By scrapping PT&R for employees the newly created franchising director was empowered to transfer workers to new subsidiaries and change contracts. The creation and eventual flotation of Railtrack, which was not initially part of the privatisation legislation, demonstrated how the earlier promises of 'no plans' for redundancies and contracting out were just hot air.

---

PT&R conditions of service were all broken up. Originally you could transfer anywhere in the industry. You could seek a job anywhere in the industry. If you were made redundant it was a question of last in, first out. We had very good promotional and redundancy arrangements. People were promoted on seniority, you didn't have this 'blue eyed boy' syndrome. That was all destroyed prior to privatisation, because it was absolutely essential that the private companies did not have the conditions that we enjoyed. When privatisation came you were stuck in that particular company, you couldn't move. If you were made redundant in that company you were made redundant. You couldn't seek alternative employment in the industry. That was a tremendous blow.

Mick Atherton

---

The outcome of the 1993 strike was a setback to the fight against privatisation and the defence of the membership. The vindictive ending of automatic check off by BR plunged the union into a financial crisis. The merger of the NUR and the NUS in 1990 had left the union's accounts in deficit, as shipping companies received payouts in damages dating back to the P&O strike. In the aftermath of the ending of check off and privatisation the union's membership sank dramatically from more than 105,000 in 1992 to 59,000 by 1995.

The break up of BR as an integrated nationalised industry had begun. In June 1993 BR Chairman Bob Reid announced that the profit centres created under the 'Organising for Quality' initiative were to be reorganised into business units based on a separation of infrastructure and operations. BR was to be broken up into a ragtag of separate entities, each with its own management and bargaining structure. Separate operating companies were formed out of various BR business units, with operations franchised out using trains leased from separate rolling stock companies. In addition separate companies were formed for advertising, signalling, telecommunications, track maintenance and renewal.

---

It was obvious that they were getting ready for privatisation, trying to make the companies look attractive. But there were people trying to get out as well, even the bosses. Many of the more experienced in the engineering side of the industry wanted out. There was a lot of turmoil. We were all fearing this efficient new organisation, and it never really materialised. If anything it was the exact opposite, there was so much unrest and upheaval. The bosses were in a state of turmoil. A lot of them were trying to make the industry leaner. It didn't work. There was so much fear among the workforce because it was quite clear within the infrastructure there was going to be a hell of a lot of job losses. If you think of all the tradesmen that the industry used to have – BR had its own carpenters, bricklayers, electricians, thousands of regional shopmen. It was quite clear that work was going to go out to anybody, to private tender. Railway electricians don't exist anymore. Everybody could see what was going to happen. If you were in one of those jobs you knew you were going.

Mick Atherton

---

It was during this period that the workforce became increasingly aware of what lay ahead. With the splitting up of assets and the separation of groups of workers into separate working units, there was widespread demoralisation. Thousands left the industry. A previously nationwide network of skill and talent, drawn from years of experience and careful progression through professional grades, with the possibility of promotion and transfer within BR, gave way to fragmentation and isolation.

In all, BR was carved up into more than a hundred separate units. A new state-owned company, Railtrack, was created in April 1993 as a track authority – charged with maintaining and repairing infrastructure. Initially Railtrack was to be maintained in public hands, but in a last

> We had the area supervisors, the true passionate railway leaders, who prided themselves on the areas they looked after. These were the ones who were going to be the most vocal against the process of privatisation. They all went. They just disappeared. The last one I knew was an Irish chap, very strong will power, well respected. He went to draw his wages in '93 and he turned to me after a meeting and he said 'I'll let you know now I've just put in for my redundancy. I can't witness this.' Not that he had had enough or felt beaten; he just was not prepared to take it. It was a sad era, to see people of that magnitude, walking away.
>
> Trackworker, Midlands Region

gasp of privatising fury this too was hastily sold off before the Tories were booted out of office in 1997.

## The Signal Workers' Strike of 1994

Having failed to halt the initial process of privatisation the union sought to defend what leverage it retained. It aimed to protect its negotiating position by fighting to maintain conditions and bargaining powers for its members. Now faced with the prospect of having to negotiate separately with the new fractured companies the union took up the cause of the signal workers. In the spring of 1994, as the government hurriedly tried to sell off the rolling stock and operating franchises, the union sought to open a broad front of industrial action aimed at pressuring the newly created Railtrack, which took over in April 1994, into industry-wide agreements to maintain workers' rights and conditions, especially in rates of pay, working hours and pensions.

One group of railway workers whose position was to be particularly affected by privatisation were the signal workers. New technology introduced since the late 1970s had greatly improved productivity, but at the cost of the loss of thousands of jobs shed in the move from manually operated signal boxes to larger multi-manned power boxes. Cable alarm systems, pagers, teleprinters, automatic train reporting equipment, computer driven communications systems, portable data terminals, touch screen telephones were all added to signal boxes in the following decade. New equipment greatly enhanced signal workers' responsibilities. Yet signal workers' wages were graded according to a complex points system based on traffic flows and equipment at each signal box, a system which dated back to the 1920s. Wages lagged behind comparable work in other grades, and the differentials between signal workers and other railway workers had narrowed accordingly. Unlike other grades in the union who had restructuring imposed on them, the signal workers had actively sought restructuring since 1987, despite the NUR executive's opposition. The union's executive sought to win the interim increase before going forward with restructuring, in accordance with at least seven resolutions of the signalling grades conferences held since the late 1980s. Negotiations with the BR board took place on this issue from 1992 until Railtrack took over direct negotiations. Railtrack for its part wanted to assert its powers as the new employer. Under Sir Bob Horton, a former chief executive of BP with a reputation for arrogance, Railtrack sought to flex its muscles against the union. The RMT tried to negotiate with Railtrack for an 11 per cent interim increase in recognition of increased productivity prior to entering into negotiation of a restructuring of the grade, but was rebuffed by BR and Railtrack which insisted that any new money – a derisory 2.5 per cent was offered – be conditional on the outcome of restructuring.

In response the RMT announced a strike vote in late March. The signal workers, who did not have the reputation of being the most militant grade in the union, voted by a four to one margin (2,531 to 566 on an 80 per cent turnout) for strike action in a series of weekly 24-hour stoppages. A thousand BR signal workers who were not part of the union were not balloted. After the vote was announced the two sides took part in 19 hours of talks over the weekend between 6 and 9 June. During the talks it appeared as though Railtrack was willing to revise its offer to 5.7 per cent. But the revised offer was hastily withdrawn at the direct intervention of Transport Secretary John Macgregor who privately insisted that BR and Railtrack stick to the government's anti-inflationary public sector pay norms. After the talks broke up, BR and Railtrack denied that the 5.7 had ever been on the table. Embarrassingly this position became impossible to maintain after Jimmy Knapp got hold of a leaked internal company memo by Colin Hall, one of BR's chief negotiators and director of the southern region, referring to the 5.7 per cent offer. Bob Horton compounded the error when he dismissively referred to the memo as written by 'an over-zealous, very junior employee'. Only later did it become clear that the government's intervention had scuppered a deal.

Last minute talks to avert a strike broke up in acrimony after only seven minutes on 13 June. Knapp denounced as 'absolutely reprehensible' the behaviour of Railtrack in negotiations: 'I have never known anything like it in my thirty years experience in the rail industry... the Railtrack board has destroyed what integrity there was in negotiating procedures, which are now in tatters. We have no faith in them.' The first of twelve weeks of industrial action began at midnight on Tuesday 14 June. Support for the strike was overwhelming. Between 80 and 90 per cent of the signal workers stayed out throughout the strike. The travelling public took the opportunity on the first day of the strike to stay home and enjoy the mid summer sunshine, and public opinion, ambivalent at best about privatisation, was shown in polls to be consistently hostile to Railtrack and the government. Both sides submitted their case to ACAS. Railtrack made a three part offer of 6 per cent, a £200 one-off lump sum payment and a projected long-term restructuring settlement worth between 13 and 26 per cent. The RMT stuck to its basic demand for 11 per cent prior to any restructuring.

The attitude of the Labour Party, enmeshed in the fraught leadership contest which followed the sudden death of party leader John Smith, was in the beginning at best ambivalent. On the eve of the first day of action, transport spokesman Frank Dobson offered no comment, while acting leader of the party Margaret Beckett refused to support the strike in the Commons. John Prescott, who was sponsored by the RMT and had been Labour's transport spokesman up until the year previously, claimed 'I am not the transport spokesman ... I do not know the full details', though he called for negotiations and blamed the dispute on the government's intervention on pay. Leading contender for the leadership and home affairs spokesman, Tony Blair, also did not volunteer any support: transport was not part of his brief. After several weeks of one day strikes the issue became the subject of heated debate in the Commons. Prime Minister John Major challenged acting leader of the opposition Margaret Beckett to condemn the strike, labelling her 'the striker's friend' for failing to do so. At the union's annual conference in Liverpool in late June Frank Dobson was more outspoken: 'the government has been demanding that Labour should condemn the strike. We refuse to condemn it. Workers who are being swindled out of

their wages have a fundamental human right to withdraw their labour.'
Throughout the strike Labour maintained that the action was avoidable
if the government had not intervened to block the 5.7 per cent deal.
Beyond this the party did not give explicit support for the strike.

The mid weekly one-day strikes dragged on through July. In the midst
of the dispute both the RMT and Railtrack were called to give testimony
to the Common's Employment Select Committee. The Committee's
Chairman Grenville Janner succeeded in persuading Jimmy Knapp
and Robert Horton to hold brief face-to-face discussions, but these
failed to break the impasse. Later the Committee heard confirmation
from Transport Secretary John MacGregor that the government had
intervened to halt the 5.7 per cent offer. Shortly after his appearance
MacGregor was replaced by the more hardline Brian Mawhinney. It
emerged that the government had set up a committee to monitor the
strike. Members of the No. 10 Policy Unit attended Railtrack meetings
and gave advice. Railtrack launched a 'hearts and minds' campaign
designed to appeal directly to the signal workers over the heads of
the union. A special hotline was established by Railtrack to enable
wavering strikers to phone in and get the company line. Railtrack
spent almost £200,000 on public advertising designed to weaken public
support for the strike and undermine the strikers' case. The right wing
press made much of the supposed return to the 'bad old days' of trade
union militancy. 'The dinosaurs are not extinct' screamed the Murdoch
controlled *Sunday Times*. Rent-a-quote Tory MPs came forward to
advocate the mass sacking of the signal workers, in emulation of US
President Ronald Reagan's dismissal of striking air traffic controllers.
The Confederation of British Industry called for a new law to ban
strikes in essential services.

Railtrack progressively managed to increase the number of trains it
ran on each successive strike days by putting pressure on the signalling
supervisors, who belonged to TSSA and the RMT, to work the signalling
boxes. Strict training in safety procedures was ignored in an effort
to break the strike. TSSA and RMT signalling supervisors protested
through their unions. Anonymous reports surfaced of supervisors
manning signal boxes with as little as one week's training.

In an effort to protect RMT members in supervisory grades from
victimisation for refusing to help break the strike it was decided to
ballot RMT signalling supervisors on joining the action. They voted

225 to 157 on a 72 per cent turnout to reject strike action. In retrospect this was a turning point in the strike. Henceforth it became difficult for RMT supervisors to refuse to work the signal boxes and left the signal workers feeling isolated from these workers in their own union. The failure of the signalling supervisors' ballot demonstrated that the union still suffered from organisational weaknesses, and artificial divisions between grades.

> People were not getting involved enough. Our regional councils were not involved. The signal workers felt that they were somewhat isolated. Some of the regional councils were useless. I remember going to one meeting and the strike was not even on the agenda. I took these signalmen in right off the picket line and I said 'look, brothers, these are striking signalmen, do you know them?' That was true in a lot of areas.
>
> Mick Atherton

On 8 August, four days after the signalling supervisors' ballot became known, Railtrack delivered an ultimatum on signal workers' pensions. Unless the restructuring of the grade was agreed to by 30 September, Railtrack stated that the signal workers' share of the BR pension fund, worth some £65 million, would be spread across the whole industry. The threat to withhold an increase to pensions upped the ante in the strike. The BR board stepped into the dispute, putting at Railtrack's disposal the names of hundreds of retired signal workers, quickly dubbed as 'dads army' by union wags, to be recruited to work on strike days. By the time of the TUC conference in Blackpool in early September the strike was still fairly solid, but morale was beginning to weaken as it became clear that, with Railtrack managing to run more and more trains on each successive strike day, a settlement of some kind would have to be reached. The Blackpool conference was full of dramatic resolutions, speeches and rallies in support of the strike. Jimmy Knapp made a rousing speech which was cheered to the rafters. John Prescott told a fringe meeting that the Tories were intent on prolonging the strike into the party conference season as a means of sustaining their anti-trade union agenda and damaging the prospects of the Labour Party. Shadow employment minister Anne Clwyd said of Railtrack boss Robert Horton, 'he is the Eddie the Eagle of big business

– incompetent, graceless and doomed to be remembered as a sick joke'.
Tony Blair, attending his first TUC conference as leader of the Labour
Party, pointedly refused to back the strike, expressing 'considerable
sympathy' for the justice of their cause, calling for arbitration to find a
settlement and stating a policy of strict neutrality: 'If I started interfering
I would be doing precisely what I have criticised the government for
doing.'

With the strikes in their fourteenth week and the pensions deadline
hanging over them a meeting of signallers was called under the auspice of
the National Signalling Grades Conference in London. The conference
president told the meeting:

> 'The whole trade union movement is now behind us, willing us on to victory,
> particularly the public sector unions. But now it goes deeper than us versus
> our employer in a dispute over a wage claim. It's become political. The
> moment the government stepped in to the dispute it became a different
> ball game ... we have picked up the banner and sword and become the
> champions of the trade union movement, of different organisations, of
> fringe political parties, in fact of the whole working class population of this
> country. All of them wanting us to give the Tories a bloody nose.'

The mood of the signallers was becoming restive. The strike had been
going on since mid June with little sign of a positive outcome. Each
week Railtrack alleged greater success in running trains to break the
strike. Railtrack was claiming to be able to run over half the normal
levels of service during the early autumn strike days. Many strikers were
thousands of pounds out of pocket. Though overall support remained
solid, in some areas resolve was weakening and picketing became
necessary for the first time to hold the line. With the pensions deadline
looming the grades conference voted unanimously for a motion in
favour of directing the EC to pursue a twin track policy of seeking
an interim payment while separately seeking to negotiate a settlement
on restructuring, with the final deal subject to a referendum of signal
workers. By hiving-off these two issues the way was cleared for ending
the deadlock with Railtrack.

The union immediately restarted separate parallel talks on restructuring
and the pay claim in haste to meet the 30 September deadline. Strike
action was not suspended, and on 21 September the Traincrew Grades
Conference voted to widen the dispute, the same day that the union
resumed direct talks with Railtrack via ACAS. What proved to be the

last day of strike action went ahead on 23 September, timed to coincide with a separate 24-hour strike on the London Underground, as some 70 hours of talks took place. A compromise deal was formulated and, in what was a unique and controversial move, the union organised a telephone referendum amongst the strikers. Over 85 per cent of those polled (on a 71 per cent turnout) endorsed the deal. The four month dispute, involving 4,000 signal workers in some 17 days of 24-hour strike action ended a little before midnight on 30 September when the union notified Railtrack of its agreement to the terms hammered out at the ACAS talks.

> It was fairy successful, even though towards the end there were some cracks starting to show. It's extremely difficult to picket in the rail industry. It's not like standing outside a factory gate. You can get into a signal box from all sorts of angles. You can't stand outside a signal box. There was one quite successful picket at Tipton Crossing where it took them some time to open the box but they had to get managers in to open the box. It was just a crossing box. But of course if this box was shut nothing could go either side of it because it was a level crossing box. Strategically it was quite an important place. There was quite a successful picket there on a number of occasions. It was recognised that this was the one group of workers who could bring the whole group to a standstill.
>
> Mick Atherton

Even though six months after the strike the bosses were attacking their gains, the signal workers did well out of the deal. The agreement which ended the strikes involved grade restructuring, the rolling up of allowances into basic rates of pay, the introduction of cashless pay, new premium payments, reduced working hours, longer holidays, individual job evaluation and seemingly generous lump sum payments, equivalent to the original 5.7 per cent offer. The union persuaded Railtrack not to include Sunday as part of the normal working week. There was however some deep concern at activist level at the method used to consult the signallers before calling off the strike. At the Annual General Meeting an angry debate took place over the whole way in which the union had conducted the last phase of the strike and the deal that ended it. It was denounced as having 'more strings in it than the London Philharmonic Orchestra'. Great concern was understandably expressed at using the telephone to arrive at democratic decisions. Yet a grade of workers that by the nature of their work are in isolation from each other were brought together by the union to fight. The signallers had shown that by sticking together they could make advances against great odds and the overwhelming majority saw the result as a victory.

BR was dismembered like a butchered carcass. First to go were operations. In the course of 1995 Intercity, Network Southeast and Regional Railways, employing around 47,000 staff, were split up into some 25 train operating companies. These were then sold as franchises to a variety of private sector companies. After several failed management buy outs the main beneficiaries of the franchises were the big bus companies which had carved up the municipal bus services in the 1980s. Stagecoach, the predatory bus company which had done so well out of privatisation of urban buses, got the franchise for South West Trains in February 1995. Stagecoach had been the subject of numerous complaints to the Office of Fair Trading for predatory pricing in its running of urban bus services. In 1995 a Monopoly and Mergers Commission condemned the company for its commercial policies at Darlington. First Bus, Sea Containers, National Express and the newly created Prism rail, a bus consortium, acquired four of the franchises. BR telecommunications, covering around 3,000 workers, was sold to the defence electronics company Racal for £133 million. Racal eventually sold on this business to the French defence and electronics giant Thales. Red Star parcels was sold to a management buy out for a nominal £1 and almost immediately made over 250 staff redundant. Freight operations were split up prior to privatisation into Loadhaul, Mainrail freight and Transrail Freight, and in 1996 were snatched up by union busting US rail company Wisconsin Central, which had already bought up BR's mail services and the Royal Train. Wisconsin Central then reconsolidated these into English, Welsh and Scottish Railways (EWS). Freightliners, BR's specialist container business, was sold to a consortium. The splintering of BR into different operational units was riddled with absurdities, creating false barriers between lines of railway work which never existed under the old system, and which made efficient operations and maintenance almost impossible.

The BR S&T department was split in half. The 'S' disappeared from the 'T' which caused all sorts of managerial problems. It was very difficult to have a department which had been together for generations, dependent on the other, split into two. There were ludicrous work situations. We always looked after line-side telecommunications and they decided we would no longer look after the telephones, but would still look after the signal box end and the lines to the telephones. We would go to a line-side telephone failure and if it was a telephone we couldn't even look at it. We couldn't repair it. We would then have to report it back to somebody else and because of the contractual way privatisation worked we could not touch it, even though we had been looking after them for years. I worked for Racal and the phones were up to Jarvis, even though they had no telecommunications skills as such. It was ludicrous. Everything became less efficient. You had the situation where you were one minute working for British Rail in the S&T department and then were going into some newsagent's shop looking after some machines for paying a gas bill, because Racal was taking on new contracts, going to prisons and taking over telephone exchanges in the street.

Mick Atherton

Control of rolling stock, comprising more than 11,000 locomotives and coaches, was transferred to three Rolling Stock Leasing Companies or Roscos. Named Porterbrook, Angel and Eversholt after the various streets where their BR offices were located, the Roscos were sold in November 1995 to management buy outs for £1.8 million. Porterbrook was sold on in mid 1996 to Stagecoach Holdings Plc for £825 million. Later on Angel and Eversholt were sold to the Royal Bank of Scotland and HSBC respectively. Abbey National, the bank and building society, later purchased Porterbrook from Stagecoach.

British Rail's engineering arm, employing some 40,000 permanent way workers responsible for the upkeep of tracks, were split up into six renewal and seven maintenance arms, known as Briscos. As an incentive to their sale the Briscos were given commercially advantageous exclusive seven-year contracts with Railtrack. As part of the fattening-up process prior to sale the contracts were deliberately loosely drawn up to the advantage of the contractor. The 13 Briscos were swiftly bought up by several multinational construction companies with little railway experience, including Tarmac, Jarvis and Balfour Beatty – all companies with poor records of union recognition, health and safety standards and close links with the Conservative Party. As has been seen, one of the main motivations for the separation of the Briscos was the break up of the union's ability to negotiate nationwide agreements.

The rump of the nationalised industry, Railtrack, was the last bit of BR to go. Not included in the 1993 Railways Act, Railtrack was responsible for the network's 11,000 miles of route track, 2,500 stations and some 40,000 bridges, viaducts and tunnels when it was created in 1994. Initially envisaged as a publicly owned infrastructure provider, contracting with the Briscos for work on maintenance, renewal and repair, Railtrack was quickly fattened up with debt reductions, concessions on the profits from the sale and development of BR property and other special arrangements which allowed Railtrack to maximise its profits at the expense of investment in railway infrastructure.

---

Different contactors were opposing each other, not interlocking. One was trying to beat off the other. As you were transferred from one company to another we were chucking brand new gear into skips because we didn't want another company to get the assets. When we went from Balfour Beattie to Serco Rail Maintenance the supervisor on the last day he became a policeman seeing we didn't take our tools to the company. When we went to work for Serco we told them what we needed. We asked for ballast forks, and they went and got garden forks. We told them we needed cross levels, they went out and got spirit levels. It was an absolute joke. You could get lost in the infrastructure, and no one would know. I've seen gangs of contactors turn up, watch them sit, all day, doing nothing. Then leave, come back the next day. I said 'why do you turn up to do nothing?' 'I don't know', he said, 'but we're paid.' If somebody had cocked up on a contract, the job didn't go out, they would do nothing. Years ago if something went down you would have been redirected to assist somewhere else. But of course you couldn't do that, you couldn't go and assist the guy in a length down the track because there was no contract in place.

Track worker, Midlands Region

---

At the same time, outright opposition by the Labour Party to the privatisation of BR gave way to tacit support for the process. The promise of complete re-nationalisation was unceremoniously watered down. Though Clare Short's outspoken promise that there would be 'no gravy train for fat cats' sounded good and may have put off bidders for the rolling stock companies (and driven down the income from the sale), re-nationalisation was effectively dumped once the first sales of BR's component parts went ahead, though in public the rhetoric of the Labour Party leadership altered almost imperceptibly. As late as autumn 1995 the Labour Party conference voted overwhelmingly for a motion, promoted by the RMT and its sister unions, which committed the party to re-nationalisation. The crunch came in the run up to the sale of Railtrack. At first party spokesmen appeared to hold the line against the sell off. A Commons motion put by the party early in 1996 challenged the sale on the basis that it was not part of the original privatisation legislation. A proposal to block the sale of Railtrack, by announcing that any incoming Labour government would exchange shares in the privatised Railtrack for preference shares, was dropped at the insistence of shadow chancellor Gordon Brown, who refused to commit incoming Labour to any future increase in public spending for the first two years of a new government. By April 1996 Clare Short announced that blocking the sale of Railtrack would be 'irresponsible'. Outright re-nationalisation was replaced by the vague promises that an incoming government would act 'dependent on the availability of resources, and as priorities allow, seek, by appropriate means, to extend public ownership and control'. A final chance to retain a measure of public ownership of urban commuter networks was abandoned when Clare Short's successor as Labour's shadow transport minister, the Blairite loyalist Andrew Smith, blocked the opposition of Labour controlled Passenger Transport Executives, which ran commuter railways in West Yorkshire, Greater Manchester and Tyne and Wear, to the franchising of these services.

The retreat by Labour from the public commitment to undo the damage of privatisation of the railways was but one aspect of a wider ideological shift. With the election of Tony Blair as leader following the death of John Smith Labour was re-branded as 'New Labour', as though a hundred year old political tradition was like a box of soap. Tony Bair's election signalled a wholesale abandonment of much of Labour's past.

It is arguable how far back this process went. After the 1987 defeat of Labour there was a gradual retreat from the aim of repealing all the

Tory anti-trade union legislation. Throughout the early 1990s a group of so-called 'modernisers' within the party hierarchy continually pushed for Labour to further distance itself from the trade unions. The 1992 Labour Party election manifesto promised to retain legislation that ended the closed shop and mandated pre-strike ballots. Much of the impetus for retaining the Tory legislation came from newly appointed employment spokesman and rising star of the modernisers' faction, Tony Blair. Under John Smith, Labour implemented a reform of the role of trade unions at the Labour Party conference, in the selection of parliament candidates and in the election of members of Labour's NEC as well as leader of the party which resulted in a reduction of the bloc vote in favour of a system of one member, one vote elections, or OMOV. Hailed by the modernisers as a triumph for democracy and by much of the Labour Party and trade union left as a betrayal of party traditions, the reform of the bloc vote was the least contentious of John Smith's reforms. There was nothing inherently socialist in the bloc vote. Indeed bloc voting had been introduced into the TUC in the late 1890s by larger textile and mining trade unions, which then supported the Conservative and Liberal parties, as a means of stifling support for independent labour candidates, many of whom came from the RMT's predecessor, the ASRS. Though introduction of OMOV may have weakened the say of the unions within the party it did not end it entirely. It was only after John Smith's death in May 1994 that the modernisers' campaign to destroy the links with the past got into full flow.

Tony Blair's leadership campaign and the speeches and policy pronouncements that followed could leave few in doubt where 'New Labour' stood in relation to the unions. Just prior to his election as leader he declared: 'Trade unions will have no special or privileged place within the Labour Party.' In a *New Statesman* article written just after his elevation to party leader he wrote: 'It is in the unions' best interests not to be associated merely with one party. The influence of trade unions will come from being a broad voice of working people, not a direct party political voice or one that is concerned for the narrow interest of individual unions.' In an *Observer* interview he intoned: 'Nobody believes in this day and age that the business of the Labour Party is to be the political arm of the trade union movement.'

In policy terms Blair's election signalled a retreat from the very modest aims of the Labour opposition during the Thatcher and Major era. There was to be no repeal of even the most egregious Tory anti-trade union laws. Employment policy, as drawn up by Stephen Byers and David Blunkett, was to stress the maintenance of a so-called 'flexible labour market', one in which bosses had the maximum powers to hire and fire at will. During the 1996 London Underground strike employment spokesman David Blunkett even suggested outlawing strikes through binding arbitration and proposed compulsory re-balloting of striking union members a few months later – an idea put forward by the Confederation of British Industry during the 1994 signal workers strike and rejected by the Tories as unworkable.

Nowhere were the lines between New Labour and the unions more starkly drawn than in the battle to ditch Clause Four of the Labour Party constitution. Clause Four committed the party

> 'to secure for the workers by hand or by brain the full fruits of their industry by the most equitable distribution thereof that may be possible upon the basis of the common ownership of the means of production, distribution and exchange and the best possible obtainable system of administration of each industry or service.'

Though Clause Four was originally adopted in 1918 as a compromise statement drawn up to satisfy the various left and right tendencies within the Labour Party at the time, for a large number of trade unionists it came to symbolise a social ideal, epitomised in the great nationalisations which followed the Second World War, of a more just and equitable society. Labour in office had often honoured Clause Four more in the breach than in the observance, and few would claim that the governments of the 1960s and 1970s were very actively pursuing these ideals. Yet the symbolism of its language, a mixture of socialist idealism and committee-speak jargon, was a benchmark by which socialists could measure the progress of the cause of Labour.

It was thus for its symbolic value that Blair and the modernisers sought to excise Clause Four as a key element in their campaign to transform the party into a media friendly electoral machine. The scrapping of Clause Four, announced in late 1994, took a full year to be pushed through the Labour Party's constitutional mechanisms, through special conferences, and was fought tooth and nail by many rank and file trade unionists, including members of the RMT. Nationally the RMT supported all campaigns to defend Clause Four and Knapp argued for its retention at the special Labour Party conference. Though his speech was a half hearted and narrow defence of the union's desire to re-nationalise the railways, as if this was the only understanding his members had of the clause, ultimately it did not matter. Blair would never have pushed the issue of junking Clause Four this far if there had been the remotest chance of losing the vote. The fear of appearing disunited in the face of a looming election persuaded many to go along with the change in April 1995. A new clause, with an even higher jargon level than the old, promised that the Labour Party would work for 'a dynamic economy ... in which the enterprise of the market and the rigour of competition are joined with the forces of partnership and co-operation to produce the wealth the nation needs'. The success of Blair in scrapping Clause Four propelled him to success in the eyes of the media and big business, and helped to ensure the overwhelming victory in the general election of May 1997. Yet the price of Blair's victory was heavy. A generation of activists, raised in the bloody onslaughts of the Thatcher era, worked hard for a Labour victory and were heartily looking forward to seeing the back of the Tories after 18 years, whatever their misgivings about Tony Blair's leadership. Others, including some RMT activists, disgruntled at the abandonment of Clause Four, joined Arthur Scargill's ill-fated attempt to form a breakaway Socialist Labour Party. Even for those RMT members who remained loyal to the Labour Party the victory of 1997 was bitter sweet. The Tories had been thrashed at the polls, but perhaps the most right wing Labour government in its 100 year history had come to office pledged to largely continue their legacy. The ideals of the party of labour, only imperfectly realised at the best of times, but the core of a tradition that stretched back to the very beginnings of the union's history, had been heaped on the pyre.

# 7
# New Labour in Power

Ironically for a cabinet that had over seven ministers who were sponsored by the RMT, the first Labour government in 18 years won the 1997 election on a manifesto that promised little change in transport policy. The words of the manifesto on transport, 'Our task will be to improve the situation as we find it, not as we wish it to be', boded ill for all those in the industry who held out hope that the May victory would usher in a new era in public transport. New Labour in power proved to be little different from what had come before. Bold promises of an integrated transport policy, overseen by the Deputy Prime Minister and former trade union activist John Prescott, proved hollow as a succession of transport ministers came and went, just as they had under the Tories. During the first four years after 1997 there were no less than six changes in the transport portfolio: Gavin Strang was replaced by John Reid who in turn was replaced by Helen Liddle who in turn was replaced by Gus MacDonald who in turn was replaced by the hapless Stephen Byers. The post only achieved a degree of stability in May 2002 when Byers resigned and was replaced by Alistair Darling. A supposedly beefed up rail regulator, the Strategic Rail Authority, was set up in 1999 but it did little to make good the disaster caused by rail privatisation and nothing at all to improve conditions for those working on the railways. A much-vaunted Ten Year Plan for Public Transport was announced in 2000. Though it made grandiose promises of an integrated transport system with a massive shift from road to rail, the plan offered relatively little in the way of new public investment and in fact merely restored investment to pre-privatisation levels. The government continued to pour public money into the private coffers of the rail operators to prop up an increasingly fractured network. It perpetuated the work of the Tories by issuing new franchises from the spring of 2001. In the dash for profits the decline in safety standards led to almost inevitable tragedies. A freight derailment at Bexley in February 1997 seriously injured four people. Later that year, on 19 September, a high speed passenger train from Swansea to Paddington collided with a goods train at Southall, killing four and injuring over a hundred. In October 1999 an outbound Thames turbo train from Paddington smashed into an inbound First Great Western train after it passed a poorly sited signal, killing 31 passengers and crew and causing 425 injuries. Almost a year later a poorly maintained stretch of track at Hatfield fractured under the weight of a passing commuter train, causing a derailment in which there were four fatalities and 70 injuries. On 10 May 2002 a midday WAGN train travelling from Kings Cross to King's Lynn derailed as it passed through Potters Bar station at the speed of 100 miles per hour, killing seven and causing more than 60 injuries. Jarvis, the maintenance company responsible for the line of track upon which the accident occurred, feebly claimed that the accident was caused by sabotage. These were the most visible and well publicised safety failures of the privatised railways, involving as they did fare paying passengers. The media paid less attention to the more 'routine' accidents involving railway workers, especially those involved in track maintenance. During this period the number of workers injured in track maintenance work increased alarmingly. In early 1999 it was reported by the *Financial Times* that 111 'unsafe acts' had occurred in the four weeks to November. According to Railtrack's own safety group report, two permanent way workers were killed and 58 were injured in 1998, 20 more than in 1997. Between 1999 and 2004, 37 rail workers died in work related accidents and over the same period there were 852 major injuries. The worst year was 2004 when eight track workers died in one year, including four men crushed to death on 15 February 2004 by a runaway trailer loaded with 14 tons of scrap while working on the West Coast main line at Tebay in Cumbria. While it would be misleading to attribute all the accidents that occurred in this period to the break up of BR, it was increasingly clear that privatisation was costing lives.

> Whereas under BR we had resources in abundance, with gangs of men in close proximity to each other, under privatisation, having been downsized quite ruthlessly, these resource gaps started to appear. Rather than plug that gap with manpower, fearful of the contract the managers would attempt to try to do the best they could. Safety would be the first victim in the process. You could no longer afford to build in extra lookout men for that little extra time for train warning. You couldn't do it because you didn't have the resources. Because it was a heavy physical job and every piece of equipment we used was heavy and painted yellow so it needed the majority of guys on site. Near misses were becoming more common. The knock on effect of privatisation was that management had been making decisions, dynamic assessments, on how they were going to get the job done. And usually it was at the cost of safety. But they were prepared to take that risk. It was a common saying among gaffers: 'don't tell me how you've done it, just tell me you have'.
>
> Track worker, Midlands Region

Public uproar at the folly of rail privatisation came to a head in the wake of the rail accidents but New Labour did not have the courage to re-nationalise. The 2000 Hatfield incident led to financial crisis for Railtrack, which went with a begging bowl to Stephen Byers for a bailout. Some £1.5 billion of public money earmarked for improvements to the network went instead to prop up Railtrack's share price. Yet the public cash failed to stem the slide in Railtrack shares and when the company once again sought a government bailout Byers' hand was forced. Railtrack went into administration in October 2001. Instead of taking the opportunity of re-nationalising the railways Byers opted for a half-hearted measure, transferring Railtrack's responsibilities for overseeing track maintenance to a not-for-profit public corporation, Network Rail, leaving the rest of the hodgepodge of private companies and subcontractors intact. Though the Railtrack debacle did for Byers' career as Transport Minister when it emerged that his special adviser Jo Moore sought to use the saturation news coverage of the September 11 attack on the twin towers in New York to release news of Railtrack's collapse, it did little to sort out the chaos caused by privatisation.

Worse was to follow. New Labour embarked on what was in effect a new wave of privatisation of the London Underground system. In the face of overwhelming opposition from Londoners themselves Deputy Prime Minister John Prescott launched the so-called Public Private Partnership (PPP) in March 1998. The proposal to hive-off maintenance and upgrading of stations, track and signalling to the very same companies which had been responsible for the fiasco of privatisation of British Rail was a slap in the face to all those who held out the faint hope that Labour might moderate some of its more Thatcherite tendencies.

The New Labour government did *some* things that apparently benefited trade unionists. A new statutory right for trade union recognition, tightly drawn, was implemented. Workers were given the right to be accompanied by a trade union official at disciplinary hearings. Workers could no longer be sacked if taking part in industrial action during the first eight weeks of a dispute and only subsequently if the employer could demonstrate that reasonable steps had been taken to try to resolve the dispute. Limits on unfair dismissal claims were raised from £12,000 to £50,000. Workers were given the right to 18 weeks maternity leave, four weeks paid holiday, and time off for domestic incidents. A national minimum wage, a demand of the movement since Keir Hardie's time, was implemented, albeit hedged by age exemptions and set at a relatively low rate of £3.60 per hour.

Yet these gains were offset by an acceptance of the main tenets of a Tory approach to industrial relations. Indifference to trade unionism became a badge of honour. New Labour in office did nothing to reverse the Tory anti-trade union legislation. This came as no surprise, as little action had been promised before the election. As if to add insult to injury New Labour in office went out of its way to antagonise and alienate the trade union movement. In the wake of the election the leadership made moves to denude the Labour Party's traditional structures of power. The National Executive Committee, upon which RMT Assistant General Secretary Vernon Hince sat as Vice Chair, was increasingly bypassed in favour of indirectly elected policy forums. The party conference was drained of its policy making and debating role and was reduced to a stage-managed rally where critical voices were rigorously excluded. With a massive majority in the House of Commons dissident voices could be easily sidelined. Out riders for Blair, such as Stephen Byers, publicly floated the idea of excluding trade unions altogether from the party. Little was achieved either way before Labour went to the electorate in June 2001. Despite big reservations trade unionists backed Labour and the government returned to office with an increased majority, but on one of the lowest turnouts of voters in electoral history.

The months after the second Labour victory were marked by events that were to bring the union's relationship with the Labour Party to a crisis point. The terrorist attacks on the Pentagon and World Trade Center in September 2001 pitched the world into a crisis which in the following three years was to witness full-scale military intervention in Afghanistan and Iraq. Tony Blair committed Britain to sending troops to fight alongside the US in George Bush's seemingly unending 'War on Terror'. The looming Iraq intervention, with the British government's duplicitous use of doctored intelligence to justify it, helped to galvanise opposition to New Labour. Discontent with Labour's failure to deal with the mess of privatisation and the legacy of the Thatcher years fused with disillusion over a foreign policy that committed British troops to fighting a war on behalf of one of the most right wing governments in US history. Opposition to the war in Iraq crystallised dissent within the union, as it had in the wider labour movement.

Up to this point opinion within the union was divided between those who held out some hope that the Labour Party could be won back to the values of its founding members and those who felt that the Blairite 'reforms' of the party had forever destroyed what remained of its core principles. For a union that was at the historic centre of the foundation of the Labour Party the idea of a break with Labour was one that was only reached after years of soul searching and debate. Before the 1997 election support for the party within the union had been strong. Party members were active at local branches. In 1996 the union membership voted overwhelmingly for the political fund which helped Labour win the election. Since 1993 the union had given some £153,000 to the Labour Party's general election fund and had achieved the highest density of party membership in any trade union, with over 3,000 industrial members. Half the shadow

cabinet were RMT sponsored MPs, including leading figures such
as John Prescott, Robin Cook and Frank Dobson. Though some
RMT members, including members of the executive, had joined the
Socialist Labour Party, formed by Arthur Scargill after the rejection
of Clause Four, there was little or no grassroots support for the idea
of disaffiliation. Proposals to disaffiliate at AGMs were consistently
voted down. The 1997 AGM at Great Yarmouth, held less than six
weeks after the Labour election victory, passed a resolution with only
one dissentient put up by the Darlington Branch re-affirming the
historic links between the union and the Labour Party. A proposal to
assist in setting up a Labour Representation Committee, put forward
by Sheffield branch, which would have in effect committed the union
to working for working class representation outside the Labour Party,
was also rejected.

But the writing was on the wall. The same AGM also carried a
resolution from LT Regional council condemning the 'betrayal and
treachery' of Labour MPs who had attacked the summer strike action
on London Underground. Singled out for special criticism was the
Labour deputy chief whip, Keith Hill, an RMT sponsored MP and
former political officer for the union. As the reality of a New Labour
government started to sink in, the mood in the union began to change.
Labour party membership within the union started to decline. By the
time of the historic AGM vote in July 2003 to allow branches to
fund parties other than Labour, less than a third of branches were
affiliated to the Labour Party and there were fewer than 300 paid up
party members in the union. The refusal of the Labour government
to countenance re-nationalisation or to amend any elements of the
Tory's anti-trade union laws led to increasing disillusion among the
rank and file. Many activists held out hope that at some point Labour
would revert to its principles, that Labour would at the very least
repeal some of the Tory legislation.

The partial privatisation of London Underground, announced by
Deputy Prime Minister John Prescott in early 1998, was more bitter
evidence that such hopes were forlorn. Prescott's PPP proposals
involved hiving-off the infrastructure of the Underground to different
private sector consortia that would control separate tube lines on long-
term leases (initially 15 but later increased to 30 years under pressure
from investors). In essence, it was quickly realised, PPP meant handing

over control of upgrading and maintenance of the Underground to the very same private sector engineering firms which had made such a killing by the privatisation of BR. In the run up to PPP the privateers' rogues gallery of familiar names, Jarvis, Amey, Balfour Beatty and Mowlem, were joined by British and US multinationals such as Bechtel and Brown & Root, a subsidiary of Halliburton, with atrociously poor records on human rights and labour relations. Far from halting the process of privatisation New Labour was extending it.

The sense of betrayal became palpable within the union. At the AGM at Carlisle in June 1998 speakers reminded the gathering of how only two years previously the union had heard a speech at the AGM at Ayr by the RMT sponsored shadow cabinet member Robin Cook which promised that once in power Labour would deliver a 'publicly owned, publicly run, publicly accountable' railway network. Swindon Branch put up an emergency resolution condemning the failure of the union sponsored MPs to condemn the PPP proposals. The motion also threatened to withdraw sponsorship from those MPs who refused to sign a statement condemning PPP. The Swindon motion was fiercely debated, with General Secretary Jimmy Knapp calling it 'a diversion'. Nevertheless an overwhelming majority endorsed the motion by 46 votes to 3. Thereafter Swansea No. 1 branch put up a motion which called on the AGM to condemn 'a system that allowed railways to be sold off to freebooters at knock down prices' and asked the union to declare that 'it cannot and will not continue to support a Labour government that has deserted its working class supporters and jumped into bed with its big business friends'. Other delegates, refusing to countenance a break with the Labour Party, warned against taking the union into 'political oblivion' leaving it 'shouting abuse from the sidelines'. John Milligan, speaking in support of the motion, gave one of the most vehement and vivid denunciations of New Labour. Quoting the words at the base of the statue of the great Irish socialist James Larkin in Dublin he said:

> '"they only look great because we are on our knees", that's the reality. Let's stand up and be counted and say that we want people to represent us in parliament, aye for a political agenda, but the agenda has got to be what the trade union and labour movement was formed for a hundred years ago.'

The Labour loyalist argument narrowly carried the day, and after an amendment striking out the threat to withdraw support from the Labour Party was carried by seven votes, the resolution condemning rail privatisation was carried.

Further attempts to use the union's authority to actively resist the Blairite project were fiercely resisted by party loyalists on the union's executive. Like other unions in other nationalised industries, the process of privatisation traumatised the organisational structure of the union. Within the RMT increasing disillusionment with New Labour vied with a deep-seated sense of loyalty to the labour movement. This naturally caused divisions within the union as to how to deal with the government, leading to a breakdown in trust between the union's leadership and its rank and file. There was no one tipping point in the breakdown of the relationship between the RMT and the Labour Party. Just as a hundred years previously the union's predecessors had taken a series of gradual steps that led to the foundation of the party, so now the process of dissolution of the historic link came by a series of incremental and increasingly acrimonious stages of confrontation.

The membership's sense of frustration with the Blair government was bound up with increasing anger over working conditions in the aftermath of privatisation. A fragmented network had led to the

---

The real discontent came in 1999 and 2000, when Labour had been in for a couple of years and nothing was happening. In 1997 there was still a bit of euphoria because they had only just been elected and there was a lot of expectation that things were going to turn around, though I had no illusions. But people started realising that what had been promised had not been delivered. There were two big issues; one being anti-trade union laws, which they did nothing about, but bigger than that was the whole issue of nationalisation of the industry. Because at the Labour Party conference in the 1990s John Prescott and Tony Blair had made perfectly clear, and there was no ambiguity about it, that they would be re-nationalising the railways. And of course that didn't happen. Because they were saying that people had better realise when they were buying the shares in the railway companies that they'll never see their money because we'll be re-nationalising them. And when that didn't happen then members did start to become really disaffected.

John MacDonald

ripping up of decades of negotiation machinery. The carefully created organisational structures of the union struggled to cope with the myriad of new companies and it became easier for the management of privatised companies to isolate and victimise union activists.

---

After privatisation we could no longer get on to induction courses. Union reps were excluded from workplaces. A whole new group of workers started who had grown up in the Thatcher years and who were harder to recruit. Companies would deny access and threaten unions with derecognition. Then again there was another danger of being isolated as an experienced rep. You were easily picked off. These companies could do that. They must have shared information on who they perceived to be the troublemakers. Their view of a troublemaker was of somebody who was trying to resist the downsizing of the workforce and the deterioration of terms and conditions, someone who was prepared to resist that, and prepared to organise to resist it. These people often succumbed to rather strange shenanigans. During the process of privatisation when all the consultations were happening, one very experienced colleague was laid off for having a bad knee, and he'd never complained of having a bad knee. They tried to sack him. He had to see a Harley Street doctor who told him he hadn't got a bad knee. But they wanted him out of the way for the process of consultation. And they succeeded. They kept him out of the workplace for three years while the legal fight was going on. When it was all over he got his job back, but it was all over. That individual would have been a key player in the resistance to that, and already was up to that point. Behind the scenes he was still actively involved but he couldn't attend meetings.

You'd get threats. I was threatened, on many occasions, to watch my back. We ended up having to be squeaky clean, whiter than white. You'd end up paranoid that these people are trying to draw you in to a situation that would end up terminating your employment. You didn't dare go there. You couldn't take it for granted how ruthless these companies could be. Once I was told: 'there ain't no one person that is bigger than this contract'. The reason that he told me was that I wanted to do an interview with the press over safety, and they told me if you do that we will be pressured into sacking you. They said that's almost certain. I said 'what about the truth then?' and was told 'the truth doesn't matter'. I did it anyway, but I did it anonymously.

Track worker, Midlands Region

Train cancellations, accidents and the near collapse of the network led, especially in the wake of the Hatfield crash, to an angry travelling public venting its fury at frontline railway workers. The 2000 Health and Safety Executive annual report detailed record levels of assaults on staff, with a 22 per cent increase on the previous year. There was a year on year increase in assaults throughout the years after privatisation. Between 1999 and 2004 there were 15,964 reported cases of assaults, an astonishing increase of over 58 per cent, a figure only partially accounted for by a greater willingness of railway staff to report minor incidents.

Having failed to halt the process of privatisation the RMT paradoxically began to rediscover a new found sense of strength by means of locally targeted industrial action aimed at winning improved pay and conditions. The privatised companies had in the immediate aftermath of privatisation made thousands of staff unemployed, thus creating skills shortages in crucial areas of the network. For example, the number of permanently employed maintenance staff dropped from 31,000 in 1994 to between 15,000 and 17,000 by 2000. Companies such as South West Trains found themselves in the embarrassing position of cancelling trains due to shortages of train drivers. Widening pay differentials between grades within the same companies caused anger and by 2001 strikes were on the increase.

The imposition of PPP on the London Underground further soured the relationship between the union and the government. Within 18 months of getting into office, and despite widespread popular opposition, the government pressed ahead with its plans to repeat the folly of BR's privatisation on London Underground, by contracting out the upgrading and maintenance of track, stations and signalling. It was the government's intention that PPP would begin by 2000 but widespread public opposition, legal challenges and action by the rail unions delayed the process. The absurdity of the Tory anti-strike laws, and the infidelity of New Labour in failing to amend them, was made apparent in 1998 and 1999. Strike laws prohibited industrial action based on what were judged in court to be 'political' ends. Thus strike ballots against privatisation *per se* were deemed political and the union could only take action on the specific job implications of privatisation. Two 24-hour strikes, to be held on New Year's Eve and 3/4 January 2000 were stopped when London Underground won a High Court injunction banning them on the grounds of the time taken between negotiations and the calling of the strike. New ballots were held in late January which showed overwhelming support for a walk out, and a 48-hour strike went ahead on 14 February 2000. The following May, with criticism mounting within the union against the leadership's failure to make significant headway against PPP, the union held an internal referendum amongst its LUL sections which demonstrated overwhelming opposition to the government's plans. Despite this, and in the face of near unanimous resistance from industry professionals and widespread opposition from the travelling public, PPP was pushed ahead.

The issue of PPP became bound up with an increasingly acrimonious internal Labour Party wrangle over the choice of candidate for the newly created office of London's mayor. The frontrunner, former Greater London Council leader Ken Livingstone, was excluded from the post of Labour's candidate for the mayoralty by a mixture of chicanery and backroom manoeuvring and ran for the post and won as an independent on a ticket which explicitly rejected part privatisation of the London tubes. Livingstone's victory ushered in a year-long battle with the government to stop the implementation of PPP in which the RMT gave him vocal support. It was even willing to work with Livingstone's transport czar, Bob Kiley, who had reputedly 'saved' the New York subway system but who also had a reputation for union busting and once worked for the CIA. The RMT gave fulsome support to Livingstone's campaign for the mayoralty and against PPP. Livingstone was to prove a false friend to the union, and on being readmitted to the Labour Party in April 2002 he moved rapidly to the right, calling on members to cross picket lines during the strikes on the Underground of July 2004.

With government determined to press ahead with PPP the rail unions responded by renewing industrial action. The RMT undertook a series of three one-day strikes in conjunction with ASLEF in the early spring of 2001 against the threat to jobs and safety posed by PPP. The unions sought a series of basic guarantees: no compulsory redundancies, consultation and agreement for staff being transferred to the private sector, and a new safety body involving the union. The ballot for strike action was overwhelming: members voted to strike by a majority of nine to one, one of the largest strike votes in the history of London

Underground. Legal action was launched by London Underground management using rules brought in under a Labour government the previous September requiring unions undertaking industrial action to provide details of numbers of members taking part in strikes by grade and location. The RMT with 7,500 members in dozens of different workplaces was faced with a dilemma. This blatant use of the new legislation to stymie industrial action was sanctioned in the High Court and later upheld on appeal. Thus New Labour had not merely failed to amend the Tory anti-strike legislation, it had in fact strengthened it. Like the workers in other industries that were privatised, LUL workers had to accept PPP. As the country went unenthusiastically to the polls, members of the RMT who had given £60,000 to the party to fight the election could be forgiven for wondering what they were doing supporting a government which had so brazenly forced a new privatisation down Londoners' throats.

---

If you look at London Underground, there you had a number of disputes running and you had members of parliament like Keith Hill, who used to work for us, getting up in the House of Commons and denouncing London Underground strikers and calling them all kinds of awful names. Talk about biting the hand that feeds you. That made people sit up and take notice. Not only were they doing nothing but they were actually now in opposition to us.

John MacDonald

---

Seafarers were becoming equally disillusioned with the inaction of the New Labour government. The fate of the seafarers at the turn of the twenty-first century was grim. Globalisation and the liberalisation of international trade put increasing strain on the industry. Sell offs and takeovers led to UK crews being sacked and replaced overnight as unscrupulous crewing companies, not unlike the dreaded crimps of the nineteenth century, became the main means of finding employment. The crewing agencies increasingly used temporary contracts to casualise the industry. Shipping became a classic area of 'social dumping': the replacement of workers from one country on higher wages and better conditions with workers from countries with lower wages and little social protection. Without prior warning on 7

April 1999 the entire crew of the Bibby International ship *Baltic Eider* were sent letters sacking them. Unbeknownst to them the ship had been sold to a group of German financiers and then chartered back to the previous owners, Andrew Weir. The crews were given in pay offs the equivalent of 60 days notice and 20 days compensation. In June 1999 RMT members working for Serac Maritime Crewing Ltd were sacked en masse during a stop in an Italian port and replaced with Filipino sailors. Claims for redundancy payments were ignored. When P&O European Ferries decided to charter out the *Stena Invicta* in December 1999 on the Holyhead to Dun Laoghaire route, control of the ship passed to Northern Marine Management which sacked the crew and replaced them with Polish deck hands and engine ratings. In Scotland government inaction over the European directive which was forcing through the privatisation of Caledonian MacBrayne, the state owned ferry company which provided vital services to the Western Isles, was a particular source of resentment and dismay.

The government's response to this was at best half hearted. In an effort to boost the size of the UK merchant fleet the government introduced a so-called tonnage tax, which taxed tonnage rather than shipping company profits – a form of tax relief on UK registered shipping fleets worth up to £50 million. Though the tonnage tax encouraged ship owners to re-register their fleets under the Red Ensign the government placed absolutely no obligations on the ship owners to employ British seafarers or to put non-UK crews on an equal employment footing with their UK counterparts.

The RMT argued in vain for the government to repeal section 9 of the Race Relations Act. Section 9 exempted shipping companies from the main provisions of the legislation. Under this blatantly discriminatory exemption a UK motorman on P&O North Sea Ferries might earn £20,000 per year while a Filipino Seafarer doing the same job on another ship in the same fleet would get just over £10,000. According to an ITF (International Transport Workers' Federation) survey carried out in 2002, Filipino crews on offshore support ships working in the North Sea oil industry were being paid £1,200 per month, or just over £2 per hour. Yet, with regard to the commercial interests of UK shipping owners that can only be seen as craven, the government has consistently refused to repeal section 9. As a result the already decimated ranks of UK seafarers continued to dwindle; the number of UK ratings declined by 10 per cent between 1997 and 2003. An increasingly ageing workforce was testimony to the difficulty of attracting new blood into jobs that were, at best, precarious. The average age of UK seafarers was between 45 and 50. By 2003, with the sacking of UK crews from the P&O Nedlloyd fleet, there were no longer any UK ratings left on the UK deep-sea fleet, and the total number of UK ratings was less than 10,000, a seemingly sad conclusion to a once proud and vibrant maritime tradition, and an indictment of a government unable or unwilling to buck the market.

On the national railways a similar sense prevailed of broken promises and hopes betrayed. Simmering resentment in the aftermath of privatisation boiled over as it became clear that the government had scant regard for the declining working conditions on the railways. Anger at New Labour's business friendly approach dovetailed with industrial disputes on the railways. The management of the train operating companies had since privatisation sought to downgrade the role of guards, shedding them of their formal safety responsibilities which were transferred to drivers, while forcing them to take on added responsibility for revenue collection with little or no improvement in conditions. The Ladbroke Grove disaster in 1999 had highlighted the crucial role of train crews. In the midst of the tragedy RMT members showed their mettle. Seconds after the disaster the guard on the inbound train, Colin Paton, was helping passengers escape from the wrecked trains and administering first aid to them, including the passengers on the guardless outbound Thames turbo. The drivers of both trains were dead. Just three days earlier the rulebook had been changed to give overall safety control to the driver instead of the guard. Shortly before the incident the company had cancelled a safety training day to put guards on ticket barrier duties. Also remarkable was the attitude of off duty railway workers. Two Virgin Cross Country employees, Wendella Jilbert and Mike Thomas, who were on their way to work on the inbound First Great Western train, immediately swung into action, collecting safety clips from the guards' compartment, applying them to the tracks to short circuit the line and ensure the nearby signals showed red, while using a ladder to assist passengers out of the stricken coaches. Another off duty guard, Gerrald Gough, an EWS employee on his way to work, used a fire extinguisher to save a woman passenger who had been engulfed in flames before turning

off the engine of the First Great Western train and leading fire crews
to the middle coach of the Thames train.* The railway may have been
broken up, privatised by the Tories and kept private by New Labour,
but in a moment of crisis these railway workers acted as workmates
and public servants, working as part of a collective unified team.

Yet these were the same workers who had seen their wages eroded,
and their skills and status progressively downgraded. Little wonder
that there was a rising tide of militancy amongst train crews in the
aftermath of privatisation. In 2000 RMT members in guards' grades
voted for action at 16 train operating companies but strikes were
blocked by legal challenges. By the spring of 2001 the RMT geared up
for a big push on pay, with a ten-point charter for train crew safety. By
the summer the union had managed to secure deals with several train
operating companies to preserve the safety role of guards, though
companies such as C2C and South West Trains held out. In May 2001
guards on South West Trains wrested concessions from management
after three days of strikes on the issue of uniforms and name badges.
Such was the degree of commuter rage on the privatised railways that
train crews and station staff were reluctant to be publicly identified.
Dubbed by the press 'the red waistcoat strikes', the action on South
West Trains was really about a struggle between a group of workers
in a privatised industry rediscovering a sense of self-confidence and
assertiveness after years of being pushed around, and a new brand of
Thatcherite management led by Brian Souter – the owner of South
West Trains' parent company, Stagecoach, and a right wing Christian
fundamentalist who had made a fortune in the privatisation of
municipal bus services.

Then, on 15 August, after a brave and long battle with cancer,
General Secretary Jimmy Knapp died. The death of Jimmy Knapp
came at a particularly fateful point in the history of the union and
the history of the movement. For a long period a growing section of
the union was becoming increasingly unhappy with the leadership's
softly-softly approach to New Labour. During the late 1990s the
union leadership had periodically ignored the democratic decisions
of the union's annual conference. Much of the growing opposition to

---

* Gerrald Gough was one of 47 people to receive a police commendation for
their bravery at the crash site.

We were an industrial trade union. We were used to responding to national action. If this is going to split up, how do we keep ourselves intact? How does the principle of industrial trade unionism develop itself in the aftermath of privatisation? How do we maintain it? At first because of this, and because of the anti-trade union legislation, we had this period, with divisions within the union about democratic decisions not being carried out, we were held up in rebuilding the union. You can liken it to an organisational nervous breakdown. Somebody has to look after the patient. But everybody rallied round to try and get a new climate within the union. The CFDU was designed to protect the structures of the union. We succeeded, right the way across the board, shippers, bus workers, in rebuilding our union.

Geoff Revell

Knapp's approach coalesced around a caucus of union activists, the Campaign for a Fighting and Democratic Union (CFDU).

This growing desire to revitalise the union's democratic structures was provoked by the leadership's inability or unwillingness to face off against the government's perpetuation of the follies of privatisation of transport. The Labour loyalists' emollient relationship with the Blair administration had failed to get the government to re-nationalise the railways, failed to prevent the introduction of PPP and failed to influence transport policy in any significant way.

The death of Jimmy Knapp pitched the union into a period of political uncertainty. Elections for a new General Secretary were due

I thought we were let down. I always thought we were being appeased. Over privatisation, we were told we could do nothing. We never even put up a struggle. What struggles there were were in isolated pockets, not coordinated to have any effect. We could have done it. Instead of having to talk to the media anonymously to get these stories out we could have had these stories out in the open. We were going to lose members anyway, why didn't we lose it through struggle. We were being given fights that were isolated, grade specific, rather than collective fights, across the grades through a common cause. We were appeased rather than being given the fight that we wanted to make.

Track worker, Midlands Region

to be held the following February. In the meantime the union was to be led by the EC, headed by the senior Assistant General Secretary Vernon Hince, himself soon to retire. The looming elections were also of wider significance within the trade union movement. Within the TUC and other unions, activists of all stripes watched with interest to see who would emerge as leader. Since the 1997 election the leaders of the three main unions and senior figures within the TUC had advocated going along with the main planks of Blair's social and economic policies. Much talk was given over to the idea of 'social partnerships': constructive engagement by the unions with employers to manage changes in working conditions. It is easy to understand how to railway and other transport workers the whole notion of 'social partnerships' was an anathema. How was it possible for the union to have a partnership with the very same organisations that had just been responsible for decimating the RMT's membership, for throwing thousands out of work while carving out private fortunes from a once publicly owned industry? The sense of radicalism emanating from the union's ranks right across the board seemed to mark something new. But senior figures in the TUC and railway industry observers were uneasy about the future direction of the RMT. In a long internal TUC memo, leaked to the *Guardian*, the TUC indulged their fantasy that the union was about to be hijacked by a far left group within the union centred around the leading contender for the post, Assistant General Secretary Bob Crow. The authors of the leaked memo seemed stupidly unaware that the individual members would decide who their new General Secretary would be by secret ballot. The membership didn't want more of the same. They wanted a members led fighting democratic union and were determined to get it.

The coming RMT election would decide whether the union continued the policy of the previous years or strike out in a new direction. The union under Jimmy Knapp had vehemently opposed the process of privatisation, and carried its message within the media and the Labour Party. It had also, under pressure from the rank and file, used industrial action to protect its membership and win back lost ground. But it had painfully failed to either halt the break up of the railways or prevent the extension of privatisation to new areas such as London Underground. To many in the union it was becoming clear that the policy of not rocking the boat was getting the union nowhere.

The election took place against further attacks on the union by New Labour that inevitably hardened RMT members' determination to seek change at the top. During a bitter series of strikes on South West Trains over pay the ex RMT employee and New Labour sycophant Keith Hill MP was reported to have met with South West Trains and told them to impose a settlement. South West Trains boss Brian Souter told the *Sun*: 'I will break this strike. We've already trained hundreds of staff to perform other duties.' While publicly maintaining the position that the dispute was a matter between the union and South West Trains, Downing Street made it known that it hoped Souter would prevail. As the industrial action continued Tony Blair became increasingly vociferous in condemning the strikes. In a widely trailed speech at a New Labour spring conference in Cardiff he condemned what he called the 'wreckers', going out of his way in lumping striking railway workers with public health services workers resisting his plans for the NHS.

As the RMT General Secretary election was drawing to a close the government took action that further alienated it from the union membership. In late January the government signalled its approval for the Strategic Rail Authority (SRA) to waive performance penalties on South West Trains during the strike period. This effectively meant that the government was allowing the SRA to use public money to subsidise an employer against losses incurred during lawful industrial action. In effect the government was assisting South West Trains in its attempt to break the strike. This blatant betrayal at a crucial moment in the strike was too much for the union. The day after the SRA's announcement the union executive issued a public warning that the union would withdraw constituency funding to those MPs in receipt of RMT funds who did not work actively on the union's behalf. Assistant General Secretary Bob Crow told the press, 'If they want to be sponsored, they have got to be seen rolling up their sleeves and fighting for us.' The South West Trains strikes had demonstrated that the Blair government was not merely unwilling to back a trade union in a lawful strike, but had revelled in the role of the bosses' friend, the hardened opponent of union militancy, even to the point of allowing Labour's strained relationship with the trade union movement to break down entirely.

On 8 February the RMT suspended strike action on South West Trains after agreeing to talks. The results of the election were announced in the following week. Bob Crow received 12,051 votes out of 18,560 votes cast, beating Phil Bialyk (4,512 votes) and Ray Spry-Shute (1,997 votes). Bob Crow had been Assistant General Secretary since 1993, and was one of a generation of new union leaders who, having grown to maturity in the worst years of Thatcherism, were determined to take a stand against the neo-liberalism which had infected the Labour Party. Born the son of a docker in Shadwell, East London in 1961, Crow went to work on the London Underground in his late teens as a track maintenance worker and was very soon drawn to trade union activism, eventually going on to become a tutor at Frant Place. Outspoken to the point of bluntness, Crow was widely recognised in the industry as a tough and skilful negotiator who could be relied upon to wrest the best possible terms out of any dispute. He made no bones about his communist background and the fact that he had never been a member of the Labour Party. He immediately became a bogeyman for the right wing press with attacks by the *London Evening Standard* in particular bordering on the hysterical. The frenzied mood surrounding his candidature stoked up by the right wing press may have contributed to an attack by fascists in his own home on New Year's Day 2002. Overwhelmingly elected on a platform of creating a fighting trade union that would campaign to roll back rail privatisation, the most upsetting thing about Bob Crow for the New Labour hierarchy and their followers in the TUC was his unwillingness to tow a line.

The election of Bob Crow as General Secretary was a manifestation of a new found sense of militant solidarity in the face of the betrayals of New Labour. A generation had passed since the defeats and passivity of the 1980s. Along with Mick Rix of ASLEF and Mark Serwotka of the PCS (Public and Commercial Services Union), Crow was immediately labelled by the press as part of the so-called 'awkward squad', a younger generation of more militant trade union leaders who were unafraid to outspokenly oppose Labour government policies. The outcome of the election signalled a revival of confidence on the part of a group of workers who, despite having their industry decimated by privatisation, had held on to their core beliefs and rediscovered a sense of collective hope. The more the media, New Labour hacks, and the bosses attacked the RMT and its leaders, the more the membership closed ranks. That unity attracted thousands of new members and in the following months would be put to the test.

1. NUR picket at King's Cross station on the first day of the national rail strike, 29 June 1982.

2. Executive members of the NUR showing their solidarity with ASLEF strikers with a £100 cheque during the 1982 flexible rostering dispute. Also present to show support were members of the NUM executive including Vice-President Mick McGahey, centre.

3. Sidney Weighell (right) at the Special General Meeting of the NUR in October 1982, which voted to accept his resignation as General Secretary.

4. Engineering shopmen lobby parliament against the closure of Shildon, May 1982.

5. BR engineering workers at Swindon march against threatened workshop closure, June 1983.

6. NUR members march in solidarity with striking miners while protesting against closure of railway workshops, August 1984.

7. NUS strikers outside the High Court protest against the sequestration of the union's assets, July 1988.

8. NUS members attempt to blockade lorries at Dover Eastern Dock, May 1988.

9. The P&O ferry dispute at Dover, May 1988.

10. Mass meeting of SARHWU strikers held in Johannesburg, January 1990. Alan Pottage had just given a message of solidarity and support on behalf of NUR members. Tensions were running high due to vigilante attacks. A plain clothes policeman was forcibly ejected from the back of the hall after SARHWU members saw his gun from inside his jacket.

11. General Secretary Jimmy Knapp announces the result of the ballot on the NUR's political fund, 1985.

12. Picket line at Liverpool Street on the first day of the nationwide strike, 27 June 1989.

13. Martin Sebakwane, General Secretary of SARHWU (centre) with Doreen Weppler, Secretary of Rail Against Apartheid, visiting striking railway workers outside St. Pancras Station, June 1989.

14. Wilton Mkwayi, prisoner on Robben Island for 25 years, visiting Unity House in the company of Doreen Weppler, Alan Pottage, Geoff Revell, and other Rail Against Apartheid activists, February 1990.

15. Bob Crow, General Secretary RMT, elected February 2002.

16. Track workers at Grant Rail after voting to strike for recognition, 2005.

17. Rail Against Privatisation mobile demonstration from Glasgow to London, May 2005.

# 8

# 'The Past We Inherit, the Future We Build'

The emphatic refusal of the Blair government to countenance any challenges from within the Labour Party put it on a collision course with the union that had helped to found it. The battle lines over funding, long discussed at consecutive RMT AGMs since the late 1990s, began to be drawn. The 2001 AGM at Scarborough had passed a motion that empowered the union to halt funding to RMT sponsored MPs if they failed to back union demands for re-nationalisation of the railways. This mandate for action was quietly ignored by the union leadership during the period of Jimmy Knapp's final illness, but on assuming office Bob Crow almost immediately issued a warning that the Labour government had to return to its roots or risk losing political and financial support. Denouncing the government for having 'deserted its working class roots and supporters and jumped into bed with its big business friends', he stressed that he was not arguing for the disaffiliation of the union from the party. Bob Crow and the executive nevertheless promised that unless the government changed its policies the union would no longer give money to the Labour Party.

The next move came in April 2002, when the RMT executive voted to propose a motion at the forthcoming AGM that would set up a new parliamentary group, with an open invitation extended to all Labour

MPs to join. The eight RMT sponsored MPs, including John Prescott and Robin Cook, were to be asked to join on the proviso that they undertook to campaign on four main principles: re-nationalisation of the railways, against PPP on the London Underground, action to reverse the decline of the shipping industry, and repeal of anti-trade union laws. Though new members of the RMT group would not receive direct funding from the union, under the terms of the executive's motion the RMT would withhold constituency funding from those already sponsored MPs who did not endorse this manifesto. The motion was effectively a challenge: back the union's core political aims or lose sponsorship.

By the time the AGM assembled at Southport in late June 2002 some 14 backbench Labour MPs signalled their interest in signing up to the new RMT parliamentary group; the group now stands at 21. The executive's motion, which was passed on 25 June by 36 votes to 13 against, cut £44,000 in direct sponsorship to leading MPs including John Prescott, Robin Cook and Frank Dobson. At the same time the Southport AGM voted unanimously for an emergency resolution put up by Swansea No. 1 branch that slashed direct affiliation fees from £112,000 to £12,000, a figure based on the number of RMT members affiliated to the party, put at the nominal amount of 10,000 members. It should be stressed that these motions were seen as an attempt to use the withdrawal of funding as a means of protesting against government policy, rather than as a means of disaffiliating the union from Labour. In fact a motion in favour of disaffiliation, put up by LUL signals, electrical and track branch, was defeated. Bob Crow himself told the AGM that, though patience with the government was wafer thin, 'for the trade union movement to abandon the Labour Party would be a serious mistake'.

The response to the union's cut in funding was immediate and dramatic. The day after the two motions on funding were passed at the Southport AGM John Prescott resigned from the union, after a membership dating back almost 50 years to his days as a 17-year-old merchant seaman. In a long political journey Prescott had gone from being a young militant during the 1966 seamen's strike, one of those denounced by the then Prime Minister Harold Wilson as a 'tightly knit group of politically motivated men', to becoming an ultra loyalist senior cabinet minister under Tony Blair, directly responsible for pushing forward privatisation on the Underground. Though he claimed it was 'a personal and very sad day for me', the political symbolism of one of the very few cabinet members from a trade union background severing his links with the union which had formed the Labour Party was lost on no one. On 17 July he was joined by Robin Cook, a union member since 1975, and by Labour MPs John Hepple and Hugh Bayley.

The Deputy Prime Minister's supposedly principled stand in resigning from the union did not prevent him from doggedly holding on to the keys to the three bedroom grace and favour flat owned by the union at Maritime House, Clapham, the old NUS headquarters. Prescott, who had rented the flat at a peppercorn rent since the 1970s, was caused embarrassment when it later came out that he had failed to include the flat in the register of members' interests. As a senior cabinet minister he had moved into an even larger government flat in Admiralty House in Whitehall and was granted exclusive use of the government's country estate at Dorneywood. Having tried unsuccessfully to buy the property off the RMT he fought tooth and nail when the union sought repossession of the flat through the courts after his resignation. This affair produced one of the better lines in the recent history of Labour–trade union relations when Bob Crow later told a meeting of the Campaign group of MPs: 'Reclaim the Labour Party? We can't even reclaim our flat.'

Prescott claimed at the time of his resignation that the Southport vote effectively imposed a 'loyalty test' on MPs and was contrary to his obligations to his constituents, the rules of the parliamentary Labour Party and a breach of parliamentary privilege. How fair were these charges? Leaving aside the question as to whether re-nationalisation of the railways would have benefited his constituents, or whether Prescott ever consulted the voters of Hull on the implementation of PPP, Prescott's complaint raised the question of the entire relationship between elected governments, MPs, political parties and funding from trade unions.

The express purpose of the creation of the Labour Representation Committee in 1899 was to create a fund to finance the election and expenses of MPs who would represent the cause of labour in parliament. While perhaps more honoured in the breach than in the observance this commitment to action was the animating source of the Labour

Party's legitimacy for most of its century-long history. Of course this did not mean that MPs voted under direct orders of their trade union sponsors, and indeed MPs have obligations to their constituents who send them to parliament that to a certain extent take precedence. All Labour governments since 1924 claimed to be governing on behalf of the whole nation, rather than merely carrying out the instructions of members of trade unions. Nevertheless the Labour Party was founded by trade unionists and it was surely reasonable to expect a Labour government to carry out policies which benefited trade unionists. Could this be said of the Blair government?

The question of infringement of parliamentary privilege was equally vexed. According to parliamentary tradition MPs are representatives, not delegates. Parliament, as the ultimate legislative body in the nation, is supreme. No outside organisation or institution can dictate to MPs how they should vote. Nevertheless trade union sponsorship, trade unionists exercising free choice to support the individuals or parties who best represented their interests, implied *some* degree of connection between funding and the policies being pursued by the government of the day, through the pursuit of manifesto commitments based on policies that the unions helped to formulate. Sidney Weighell, no militant wrecker, had recognised this when he threatened to withhold funding and indeed was accused of breaching parliamentary privilege in 1974. In the case of the Blair government it was very difficult to see in what sense the policies being pursued benefited transport workers in particular and the cause of labour in general. It can be argued that even at the best of times the Labour Party was never a genuine socialist party representing the interests of the working classes, though there were of course committed socialists in it. Yet even so, in the case of the Blair government any pretence of working for a more just and equitable society through a social democratic programme of redistribution and legislative reform has been so utterly abandoned as to render the whole concept of New Labour as the party of labour virtually meaningless. It is equally worth pointing out that the accusation that the RMT was crudely using the threat to withdraw money to influence the government was being levelled at a time when New Labour was becoming increasingly reliant on a string of millionaire donors, whose motives could hardly be described as purely altruistic.

The Southport resolution was seen as an interim measure, designed to satisfy both those within the union who wanted to get the government to mend its ways, to see sense, and those for whom the cause of saving the party was lost. It was designed as a temporary expedient, or as one delegate put it, the 'last chance saloon'. The new parliamentary group was to be a year-long experiment. Prescott's lofty invocation of parliamentary privilege as his reason for resigning from the RMT was rendered meaningless when the Speaker of the House of Commons ruled that the union had not breached parliamentary privilege by requesting members of its parliamentary group to sign up to its manifesto.

The 2002 Southport annual conference also mandated the RMT executive to bring forward rule changes to allow the union to support candidates outside Labour. The devolution of power by the Labour government in Scotland, Wales and England paradoxically appeared to provide the possibility of alternatives to the Labour Party. The creation of the Scottish Parliament, the Welsh Assembly and the Greater London Assembly, all elected on the basis of different versions of proportional representation and party lists, provided the opportunity for smaller political parties to gain seats in these assemblies. In Scotland, the election in May 2003 of five new MSPs of the Scottish Socialist Party, founded after the expulsion of the Militant Tendency from the Labour Party, seemed to show that socialist candidates outside the Labour Party were capable of winning elections. In the Welsh Assembly the nationalist Plaid Cymru formed the main opposition, winning seats on the basis of policies to the left of Labour. The Green Party won seats on the London Assembly on a platform of promoting public transport and against PPP. In the same election ten RMT LUL workers led by Patrick Sikorski, who was elected as Assistant General in 2002, ran as candidates as part of the Campaign Against Tube Privatisation gaining 17,000 votes. The mass anti-war mobilisation in the run up to the start of the Iraq war in 2003 seemed to point to a groundswell of opposition to New Labour. Within the Labour Party and the trade unions there was a growing movement of opposition to Blairism, with calls for a rebuilding of the party's socialist traditions from the bottom up. What role would the RMT play in these developments?

The RMT placed itself at the forefront of opposition to both the government's commitment to going to war and the main planks of New Labour's economic and social policy. Through the platforms of the TUC annual conference, where the RMT proposed a motion against the war, and the Labour Party Campaign Group of MPs, which included a large number of the newly formed RMT group of MPs, the union continued to argue its case in favour of re-nationalisation of the railways, against the looming war in Iraq and New Labour's unchecked rightward shift. The RMT group of MPs did sterling work in arguing the union's case in parliament through a series of early day motions, meetings and press briefings. Bob Crow spoke at the million strong demonstration against the war in Hyde Park in March 2003. At the 2003 Labour Party conference RMT delegates fought tooth and nail for a vote on the Iraq war, and though they were thwarted by the conference organising committee they succeeded in holding a debate which, despite desperate efforts at stage management, highlighted the depth of dissent within the Labour Party over the war. When parliament finally was given the chance to have its say on the Iraq war an unprecedented backbench rebellion took place. Up to 140 Labour MPs voted against the war after a debate which included a dramatic resignation speech by Robin Cook.

Yet the Blair government continued to face down its opponents, relying on the quiescent majority of MPs who did not rebel. In the twelve months from July 2002 the government did nothing to allay the sense of betrayal felt within the union's ranks. The bitter pay dispute involving the Fire Brigades Union (FBU), whose members went on strike in November 2002, provided further evidence of New Labour's intransigence. The RMT was especially concerned about the safety implications of the strikes on London Underground, and the union advised its members not to work on if they had safety concerns. Though LUL shut those stations accessible only by lifts it insisted that the rest of the tube system was safe. In solidarity with the firefighters RMT members on LUL took unofficial action on the issue of tube safety. At the same time, government outrageously denounced FBU strikers as 'criminally negligent' to strike on the verge of the Iraq war, echoing the ravings of the right wing press who accused the firefighters of being the equivalent of Saddam's 'fifth column'. New Labour's condemnation of the striking firefighters angered fellow trade unionists in the RMT. Transport workers looked first to firefighters and other emergency workers in the event of accidents and emergencies. At Ladbroke Grove and elsewhere, as in the 7 July terrorist attack on the London Underground, firefighters came to the immediate aid of transport workers, and members of the two unions worked together to save lives in such accidents and emergencies. The whole of the membership was appalled at the Labour government's attack on the FBU.

The continuing deterioration of the railways and the consequent threat to jobs, wages and working conditions hastened the union on its collision course with the government. In early 2003 the SRA Chairman Richard Bowker announced that the SRA was giving up passenger growth targets and proposing a series of devastating cuts in services. Over the course of 2003 a 50 per cent cut in funds for maintenance was announced. The SRA's new plans looked likely to be a creeping re-run of the Beeching cuts of the 1960s as thousands of miles of rural lines were to be downgraded to 'community rail lines' which ran the risk of being rendered unviable by neglect. In February 2003 Network Rail revealed that in an effort to control spiralling costs it was cutting £5 billion from its maintenance budget. In June Royal Mail announced it was moving its entire postal haulage services from rail to road. Prescott's ambitious plans appeared to be in tatters.

Events on the railways did nothing to stifle the growing opinion that the whole drift of government transport policy was, to put it very mildly, in apparent freefall. Throughout 2003 the union continued to try to defend members' jobs and conditions, while the Blair government connived with the SRA in handing out millions in taxpayers' money to subsidise the train operating companies during disputes. The union launched an industry-wide campaign against the downgrading of guards. Railtrack Safety, the Railtrack subsidiary which was charged with upholding the operational rulebook, had reneged on a commitment given in 2002 to write the guard's safety role into the rulebook and this situation was perpetuated when Network Rail took over from Railtrack. Strike action in defence of the safety role of guards, given renewed impetus in the wake of the Potters Bar accident, was taken at 12 of the 21 train operating companies. As was the case with the South West Trains strikes in 2002, the government gave the go-ahead for the SRA to waive penalty charges against the train operating companies on strike days to the tune of £10 million. The year-long pay dispute by conductors on Arriva Trains Northern ended when the Arriva Trains Northern membership reluctantly accepted a revised but still miserly offer. Again Arriva Trains Northern had been sustained throughout the dispute by the SRA, which bankrolled the company during the strike through waiving performance penalties.

The continuing deterioration of conditions for RMT bus drivers also compounded the union's sense of alienation from New Labour. RMT bus workers had long been fighting on issues that for many of the membership were years away. Thatcher's deregulation of the bus industry had resulted in the abolition of national bargaining under the National Council for Omnibus Industry. The bus section of the membership was broken up into individual bargaining groups that were then subject to amalgamations and takeovers. The bus membership had to reorganise itself and fight back to protect their pay and conditions. Workers in companies like Wilts & Dorset, First Devon & Cornwall, and Stagecoach Devon are among those who had the courage to fight to protect their pensions, improve their pay and maintain their conditions. Low pay in the bus industry had become a national disgrace and New Labour governments had done nothing to address the problem, yet these bus workers were supposed to believe that New Labour's continuation of the Tory policies of deregulation of bus services was in their best interests. RMT members looked on in angry despair at the fiascos committed under the Blair government in its second term. Though the RMT parliamentary group upheld the union's case within parliament, and staunch Labour loyalists, such as the union President John Cogger continued to argue the case for fighting New Labour from within, it was becoming evident that the union was at a crossroads.

The route towards disaffiliation was definitively taken at the AGM at Glasgow in July 2003. Here in an anonymous modern hall at Glasgow Caledonian University delegates gathered on the morning of the third day of the conference, Tuesday 1 July, to decide the fate of the union. Just before the conference Network Rail announced a body blow of 2,000 job cuts, a few short weeks after bonuses worth several million pounds were awarded to Network Rail senior managers. Having heard the day before highly charged speeches by

John MacDonnell, George Galloway, then MP for Glasgow Kelvin, who had recently been suspended from the parliamentary Labour Party for anti Iraq war statements, and Scottish Socialist Party convenor Tommy Sheridan, the AGM was prepared for an in-depth debate about the relationship with the Labour Party.

The motion before the annual conference, drawn up by the EC the previous March, was to amend rule 26 of the union's rulebook to read:

> 'That this union shall affiliate to the Labour Party. The Council of Executives may be, from time to time, requested by branches or regional councils to explicitly authorise support for other organisations or campaigns in pursuance of the union's policy objectives, subject to not breaching the provision of these rules. Any such request should be placed in front of the Council of Executives within fourteen days of its receipt at Head Office'.

In a dramatic two hour debate delegates wrestled with the whole issue of the link between the union and the party. Bob Crow, who kicked off the debate, made national headlines with an impassioned speech that denounced the government as 'a cabinet of war criminals' who had merely continued the work of the Tories. Speaker after speaker lambasted the bad faith of the Blair government. Many speakers reminded delegates of the historic role of the ASRS, and of how the Labour Representation Committee had been created precisely because the existing parties, especially the Liberal Party which up till then most trade unionists supported, had consistently sided with employers in industrial disputes. New Labour had become the twenty-first century equivalent of the Liberal Party in the age of Taff Vale, a party in which pious sentiments about reform and progress failed to disguise its naked class bias against organised labour and working class interests. What is striking about the 1 July debates was that even those who most fervently argued against the motion did so on the grounds that the best way to fight New Labour was from within the Labour Party. Some of the most impassioned denunciations of the New Labour government came from advocates of this position: 'This is an anti-trade union government, this is a reactionary government that is advocating Thatcherite economic policies.' No one, not even the most ardent advocates of the retention of the link with the Labour Party, was willing to defend the Blair government from the floor. Other speakers wanted to go further, and break with Labour entirely.

Though it was recognised that the resolution brought the union perilously close to outright disaffiliation it was unlikely that a motion on a clean break with Labour would have passed the conference. The motion was, therefore, a compromise. It kept the link with Labour but allowed individual branches to make their own minds up, subject to the approval of the RMT executive. Finally, in an atmosphere tense with a sense of the historic significance of the decision, delegates voted 45 to 5 to keep national affiliation with the Labour Party but allow individual branches to affiliate to organisations and parties other than Labour. Other successful motions at the AGM pointed the same way. The conference also voted to cut direct funding from 10,000 members to 5,000. At the same time the union voted to once again support Ken Livingstone's independent candidature for London's mayor.

> They kicked us out because of a resolution that was carried at the AGM. Once that happened we were then in breach of the rules of the Labour Party. And of course people did that consciously. They knew what the consequences were going to be when they carried those resolutions. It wasn't that people were ambushed or anything like that. It was explained very clearly that if you carry this is the likelihood of what will happen. And that is what did happen. The Labour Party turned around and said we were in breach of their rules and no longer wanted to know us. If you like it was an engineered thing. If you'd had a resolution there that purely said we disaffiliate from the Labour Party it may have been carried but there would have been a hell of a lot more argument about it. The atmosphere was quite tense, but there wasn't a big division there. Certainly those who were opposed to the moves we were making were very much in a minority. People knew exactly what the consequences were because they had that few days to talk about it and think about it amongst themselves. To be honest there wasn't any sort of hostility and at the end of it there was quite a bit of euphoria from the majority because we knew what that meant. We were thinking 'not before time'.
>
> John MacDonald

Labour's response to the historic Glasgow vote was at once cautious and menacing. Party General Secretary David Triesman warned the union that any affiliate that funded a candidate standing against the Labour Party was in breach of the party's rulebook but that 'it is important to be clear we are not at that point yet', while party Chairman Ian McCartney warned 'the ball is very much in the RMT's court'. The party took the exceptional step of writing directly to the 300 RMT members who were still signed up as Labour Party members and in the process sent letters to a good many lapsed members. In the aftermath of the July vote, five of the RMT's 25 Scottish branches – Edinburgh and Portobello, Glasgow 1 & 2, Glasgow Engineering, Perth No. 1, Wishaw and Motherwell – opted to support the Scottish Socialist Party (SSP) candidates, requesting the union's NEC formally approve of the move. By November the Scottish Regional Council voted to affiliate to the SSP and two more Scottish branches were on the verge of sponsoring the SSP. Bob Crow wrote to the party on 9 December requesting a meeting to discuss the threat of expulsion. The official response came in January 2004 when the Deputy General Secretary of the Labour Party Chris Lennie wrote formally to Crow. Lennie's terse letter issued an ultimatum: revoke the 1 July motion immediately or face expulsion from the party. Lennie's letter stated that the July motion had constituted 'a fundamental breach of the Rules and the essential nature of your affiliation to this party and amounts to a repudiation of the RMT's affiliation to this party' and that unless the union immediately revoked its decision of the previous AGM 'the matter will be reported to the National Executive Committee at the earliest opportunity with a recommendation that the RMT be treated as disaffiliated from this party forthwith'.

In fact, as numerous observers pointed out, the Labour Party constitution was incredibly vague on the issue of the grounds for disaffiliation of trade unions and associated organisations. Lennie's letter cited two clauses in the party's constitution that were deemed to be relevant, but strikingly neither specifically mentioned the grounds upon which affiliated organisations could be expelled from the party. Chapter 1, clause 11, section 4, quoted by Lennie, stated that affiliated organisations must:

(a) accept the programme, policy and principles of the party
(b) agree to conform to the constitution and standing orders of the party
(c) submit its political rules to the NEC.

Lennie's letter also cited chapter 1, clause 7, section 3.a which empowered the NEC to 'enforce the constitution, rules and standing orders of the party and also to take any action it deems necessary for such purpose, including disaffiliation, disbanding, suspending or otherwise disciplining any affiliated organisation or party unit'. There was no specific prohibition against supporting other political organisations, and indeed during the tempestuous mayoral elections for London in 2000 the RMT, along with several other trade unions, had openly and without threat of expulsion given money to Ken Livingstone, then running as an independent against the official Labour candidate Frank Dobson. During elections to the London assembly RMT members had run against the Labour Party on an anti-PPP ticket. Lennie's citation of that section of the party's rulebook that called on affiliates to accept the programme, policy and principles of the party, and failure to do so as grounds for ejection raised a few hollow laughs. If this rule were to be enforced uniformly there would be virtually no trade union affiliates in the Labour Party, so far had New Labour policy drifted from the trade union movement.

The Labour NEC met on 27 January 2004 to decide the fate of the RMT. No verbatim transcript of the meeting has been released but it is clear from different accounts that there was a certain degree of support for the union's position. Veteran left wing MP Dennis Skinner put forward an amendment on the expulsion motion for a special meeting with the RMT to allow the union to put its case in the hope of finding a compromise. It was pointed out that Ken Livingstone had recently been allowed to put his case directly to the NEC and been readmitted to the party. NEC member Mick Cash, RMT Assistant General Secretary and an advocate of maintaining the link with Labour, argued that the party rulebook was unclear on the issue of affiliation, and that the RMT should be given a chance to state its case. Christine Shawcroft also pointed to the vagueness of the party's rules, and the need to keep the RMT within the Labour Party. Mark Seddon also called for negotiations, and asked that the whole matter be put before a party conference. But the Blairite loyalist view was that allowing the RMT to put its case to the NEC 'would just be used for grandstanding'. This ultimately prevailed. Skinner's motion was defeated 16 votes to 7 with the TGWU supporting the motion.

In the end it was left to party Chairman Ian McCartney to put the knife in. What was wanted was 'absolute clarity', deferring the decision would merely add to the confusion. The RMT was to be made an example of, to teach other unions a lesson about the dangers of disloyalty to New Labour. In the end the NEC voted by 21 votes to 3 (the dissentients being Mick Cash, Mark Seddon and Christine Shawcroft) to expel the union from the party which its lineal parent organisation had helped to found 102 years before. With the exception of Mick Cash, none of the trade union delegates on the NEC voted against expulsion. The RMT was singled out for punishment. Nor was the union availed of the formal opportunity to defend itself, or given any right to appeal the decision. Bob Crow responded to the vote with a plea for such a hearing, telling the media that the union was not seeking disaffiliation, and pointing to the lack of natural justice in denying the union the right of appeal; as he colourfully remarked, 'even Harold Shipman was given a hearing'.

The union executive's decision to recognise the vote by the five Scottish branches and the Regional Council to affiliate to the SSP had been frozen pending a SGM on the issue in Glasgow in early February. On 6 February delegates returned to Glasgow for the special conference. This time the implication of any decision taken by conference was clear. Seven motions were put up, all but one defying the Labour NEC's ultimatum. Some called for an immediate trade union-wide campaign for reinstatement of the RMT. 'We should send a clear message that we're not going to be dictated to by the Labour Party', Bob Crow told the conference. 'No political party should tell us what to do with our money.' If the intention of the NEC vote had been to intimidate the union back into line, it backfired dramatically. After a short debate the SGM voted 42 to 8 to uphold the July decision. The expulsion order would come into effect by 12 noon the next day.

---

At the SGM at Glasgow people got up and said what they thought. We made a decision in July and now we should stick to that decision that we would decide in future where our money went, to people who supported us, not people who carried on persecuting us and speaking against us. You knew from the atmosphere and the people who were getting up to speak that the result was a foregone conclusion. There was never any doubt that our position would be reinforced.

John MacDonald

The next day, back in London, the union took part in a Convention of the Trade Union Left at Friend's House in the Euston Road, organised by the Socialist Alliance and attended by 700 delegates. Bob Crow, the first speaker, began talking as the clock ran towards midday. While praising the work of the Labour MPs of the RMT parliamentary group and promising that the union would continue to send its affiliation cheques to the Labour Party, he emphasised the sense of estrangement of the union from the whole rightward drift of the party under Blair. He pointed to the historic role of the union's predecessors in the past century of the trade union movement, and of the betrayal of that movement by New Labour:

> 'I'd rather see an independent campaigner stick up for the workers' interests than someone with a red rosette stabbing workers in the back. We were involved in Taff Vale, we were involved in the General Strike, we've supported public sector workers, nurses, ambulance workers. We never moved a cobble of coal from 1984 to 1985. We had people sacked and gave thousands of pounds to the miners. Unlike New Labour, we can look ourselves in the eye and say: "we supported the workers".'

As the clock moved towards the hour he was defiant. 'It's two minutes to go now,' he said, 'and I feel like the Birmingham Six when they got out of jail.' As the audience rose to give Crow a standing ovation, a cornerstone in British trade union history had been turned. The union that had been instrumental in the creation of the Labour Party was unceremoniously shown the door. What would the future hold?

---

Even the most non-political of our members had had it with the Labour Party. They really felt what they were doing was totally against our tradition and our interests. It was a very popular move. I don't actually know any union members who are in the Labour Party. We were virtually all members of the Labour Party at one time, we might have all belonged to various groupings, but at least most of us were members. On the EC everyone was in the Labour Party, unless you were in the Communist Party. The political climate towards the Labour Party changed both for the activists and the ordinary members. The government are going to have extreme difficulty getting our members voting Labour at the next election.

Mick Atherton

There were many who said at the time that the RMT would face political oblivion. Ian McCartney had warned that the decision had 'led the RMT out into the cold for the privilege of sitting around the table with a Trotskyite splinter group'. The claim was made that the union would lose influence, as though the Blair government had been hanging on every word uttered at the union's AGM. After the February decision the union announced it would seek legal advice to see if it could fight the expulsion and there were calls for a trade union-wide campaign for reinstatement. Affiliation to the Labour Party was and still is enshrined in the rulebook, and the union has continued to pay cheques for affiliation fees. Bob Crow told the media: 'if Labour doesn't want to cash them, it's up to them'. Though many perhaps hoped for an early reconciliation, and campaigned for readmission, it soon became clear that the union had to move on and seek an independent course in new and uncharted waters. Some made the comparison with a failed marriage, where it was best if both parties sought to put the immediate past behind.

> Our decisions at Glasgow have shown our political independence. It has shown quite clearly that we are totally serious when we say we want the industry put back into public hands. And that we are not going to pay money or support any organisation that does not go along with us on this. There was no backlash from the rank and file membership. Nobody was saying 'Oh, I think we made a mistake. We should not have done that, we were a bit rash'. People understood perfectly that we could no longer be seen to support a party that did not support us. It was a nonsense, it was ludicrous to pay people to keep laws in place that keep us down. It defied logic.
>
> John MacDonald

Outside observers looked for indications that other unions would follow the RMT out of the Labour Party. The Fire Brigades Union, stung by its treatment at the hands of the Blair government during the 2003 pay dispute, did indeed voluntarily leave the party. Other unions, such as the CWU, substantially cut funding. The Blair government, trying to make up for lost time, sought to reconcile the larger unions through the so-called Warwick Agreement, signed in the summer after

RMT disaffiliation. This agreement committed the government to a series of vague and easily watered down promises, most of which were already manifesto commitments that it had failed to act on previously. Nevertheless there was no stampede by the leadership of the larger unions to follow the RMT, though the level of disaffection in the unions with Blair grew even greater, and echoed disillusionment with New Labour in the country as a whole when Britain went to the polls in May 2005. Labour was re-elected but with a greatly reduced majority, and voter turnout was the lowest in modern electoral history. The Labour Party itself experienced a massive drop in membership as life-long supporters abandoned the party in droves. Labour Party membership fell from about 400,000 at the time of the 1997 election to about 200,000, a figure artificially inflated by the party hierarchy by means of counting lapsed membership.

In the months after the expulsion the union sought to carry on with the task of reconstructing a broad based progressive programme within the labour movement. Since then the union has continued to support efforts to fight back against Blairism outside the institutional limits of the Labour Party. This has not meant that it has cut itself off from like-minded socialists within the Labour Party and the wider trade union movement. It has given fulsome support to the foundation of the Labour Representation Committee, a campaign group formed in July 2004 with the aim of reconstituting the socialist roots of the Labour Party. The LRC whose moving spirits include the leader of the RMT parliamentary group, John McDonnell, aims to build a movement of trade unionists and labour activists who seek to renew the traditions and ideals which lay behind the creation of the original Labour Party. At the same time the RMT has given support via its branches to the Scottish Socialist Party and John Marek's independent candidacy in the Welsh Assembly. Various political groups, including the newly founded Respect coalition, angled for RMT support in England, though there has been no groundswell of support for any of these projects within the union. Instead the union has charted an independent course, working with a broad range of political organisations, civil society groups and campaigns, to fight for the cause of public ownership and control in transport, and for a more just and equitable society as a whole. Most recently the union sponsored a conference, 'The Crisis in Working Class Representation', which brought together activists from across the labour movement to debate the way forward. It remains to be seen whether the Labour Party can be rebuilt as a vehicle for achieving these aims, or whether the future lies in a newly formed party representing the aspirations of the working class as a whole. Whatever the outcome of the process of various attempts to reconstitute a left wing alternative to the neo-liberalism of New Labour, the RMT will add its powerful collective voice to all those groups and individuals who continue to fight for a society based on the values of cooperation and solidarity.

Despite the doomsayers who predicted that the expulsion by New Labour would lead to the decline of the union, the RMT emerged from the period if anything stronger. Within three months of the expulsion the union announced that it had increased its membership by 3,000. This is no doubt down to the strength of will of the membership, who have rebuilt the union from the bottom up. This did not happen by accident. The union has embarked on an ambitious membership drive, coordinated by a special organisational unit set up in 2002. The express purpose has been to recruit and train new members to be activist workplace representatives, whose aim is not merely to increase numbers but to strengthen the union's rank and file. The unit, led by Alan Pottage and based in the old NUS headquarters in Clapham, has built up a strategy that drew inspiration in part from previous experiences with SARHWU, the South African railway union the RMT supported in the struggle against apartheid. South African trade unionists had shown, under conditions far more parlous than anything faced in the UK, that a union's strength lay not just in numbers but in the degree of commitment to organising in the workplace. This strategy, dubbed 'organising for recruitment', has not only paid enormous dividends in terms of bringing the union back into workplaces from which it had been driven by the fragmentation caused by privatisation, but has also taken the union into new sectors of the transport industry in which it has never been represented.

The result has been a renaissance of representation. It has been estimated that since 2002 the union has grown by 3,000–4,000 members per year. Research undertaken by Professor Gregor Gall at the University of Herefordshire has shown that the RMT's policy of recruitment has meant that the union has grown at 6 per cent per year, making it the fastest growing union in Britain. Membership rose

In South Africa if they didn't organise they would starve. The intensity of their work was inspirational. They found solutions to the huge obstacles put in their way. The focus was on workplace organising. They would have roving meetings; they would have round the clock meetings. No effort was spared. What I learned from my time in Rail Against Apartheid and SARHWU was the importance of the rank and file element to everything that we do. That we put ourselves out, we make sacrifices to our own domestic situations to cover the country, to go to these conferences, to regional councils to explain why it is important to organise. We are trying to replicate that success.

Alan Pottage

from 57,000 to 71,000 between 2000 and 2004 and now approaches 75,000. At a time of declining overall membership in other trade unions this has been a remarkable feat. Much of the recruitment has consisted of winning back membership in those sectors where privatisation crushed morale and splintered the workforce. The union has recruited new members from amongst privatised contract cleaners and caterers, amongst the most exploited of the transport workforce. It has revived its presence in freight haulage and parcel delivery firms where it has fought a tough battle to gain access to workers. It has organised workers, won recognition agreements and improved conditions for workers across the transport industry, among sectors as diverse as rural bus services, licensed taxi firms, the offshore oil industry, and railway station catering and retailing. The union has sought to create a national network of workplace reps, with lay activists being recruited in every workplace. Since being elected as General Secretary, Bob Crow has made a point of meeting RMT members in virtually every workplace in Britain. These visits have helped to strengthen the sense of the RMT as a specialist national union for all transport workers, regardless of the sector in which they work or the size of their workplace. As part of its organisational efforts the union is on the verge of reopening a national education centre at Doncaster, a much needed resource since the sale of Frant Place which comes at a time when the TUC has closed its own national education centre.

The rebirth of industrial trade unionism within the RMT has meant that the union has been able to use its collective strength to win new

> We are not inventing any great new theories. We learned from the SARHWU experience, and that it goes back to the turn of the last century when unions started to build themselves up, they called it 'new unionism'. It's the same. You just have to roll your sleeves up and graft as hard as you can. There are not a lot of great new scientific models. We are doing the same thing our predecessors did. You have to give yourself and the organisation a shake and prioritise organising.
>
> Alan Pottage

rights for its members through judicious use of industrial action. The union has managed to punch above its weight, winning a series of disputes that have shown how, through solidarity and organisation, workers in the twenty-first century can fight back against the supposed triumphs of the market. In various sectors of the industry the union has won the right to retain a full salary pension scheme for all new workers, and the battle to defend and retain pension rights, a form of deferred wages, will continue to be a key battle to come. It has fought and won disputes that have resulted in a guaranteed 35-hour week. Employers across the sector treat the union as a serious and determined negotiator, willing and able to apply pressure where necessary in defence of its members. The union's new found strength has enabled it to extend new benefits to members. The RMT credit union, founded in May 2004, enables members to escape the crippling effects of debt from credit card companies. The union has created a 24-hour helpline to assist members with legal, financial and workplace problems. The union retains full time solicitors to give access to comprehensive legal aid in cases of compensation for industrial injury, in employment tribunals and disciplinary procedures.

Within the union the renewal of membership has been marked by concerted attempts at mobilising traditionally underrepresented and marginalised groups of workers. Advisory committees and annual conferences have sought to represent the views of women, gay, lesbian and black and ethnic minority members within the union. The union, representing a traditionally male-dominated industry, seeks actively to promote the representation of women within the RMT. Though women have always played an important and undervalued role in the transport industry, as a group women have been underrepresented in the union during a period when the number of women working in the industry has grown. Women now account for a third of the workforce across the transport sector, yet only account for just above 10 per cent of the membership of the union. To overcome this gap the RMT has sought to enhance the role of women's organisations within the union, via its standing women's advisory committee and an annual women's conference. The union has sought to campaign on issues which particularly affect women workers, such as maternity leave, child care facilities, and harassment. Each issue of the union's official publication, *RMT News*, now carries a page devoted to women members. More women are putting themselves forward for election as delegates to the annual conference. The union knows much more remains to be done to ensure that women play their full role in the life of the RMT. The reasons for strengthening women's participation in the union are obvious: the number of women in the industry will only grow in the future. Employers commonly use sexual divisions as a means of divide and rule. Women often work in some of the most poorly paid and casual sections of the transport industry such as cleaning and catering. In order for this exploitation to end the union must recruit and retain women members. In turn the full participation of women can only strengthen the union.

Similarly the RMT has sought to build up the role of black and ethnic minority members within the union through the national black and ethnic minority advisory committee and an annual black and ethnic minority conference. Though the RMT has a proud tradition of black and ethnic minority participation, there was a long struggle to overcome racial prejudice in the old railway and shipping industry. In the 1970s the NUR took a stand against attempts by racist groups such as the National Front to infiltrate the union, and more recently the RMT has expelled a number of neo-fascists who have sought to gain entry. Bob Crow has very publicly gone out of his way to identify the RMT with the struggle against racism and the far right. The union cannot afford to be complacent about what has been achieved. The vitality of the RMT as an organisation depends on its ability to draw on the talents and activism of *all* its members. The old trade union watchword 'unity is strength' is never more needed now in a society in which the politics of ethnic and racial division seek to make mischief.

The union unashamedly campaigns for its core aims of public ownership in transport, legal equity for trade unions, and social justice for transport workers on land and at sea. These aims have been fought for through active and vocal political campaigning – within the industry, in parliament and in society at large. The RMT has been at the forefront of a broad based movement for the re-nationalisation of railways, the repeal of the Tory and New Labour anti-trade union legislation, and for ending discrimination and wage slavery for international seafarers. The union has been instrumental in mobilising a number of national and international trade union coalitions, environmental and transport pressure groups in the pursuit of these aims. Internationally it has worked with organisations such as the ITF to campaign for and extend practical support to trade unionists around the world. It has campaigned on behalf of trade unionists in Colombia, opposed US economic sanctions against Cuba, and provided support for building up independent trade unions in Iraq. The RMT has worked with other maritime unions in the ITF to combat the scourge of sweatshop conditions on cruise ships and near slave labour at sea. The break with the Labour Party has not cut off the union from like-minded campaigners within the wider labour movement. On the contrary, disaffiliation has enabled the union to channel its funds to where there is the greatest need, and allowed it to speak out openly and independently, without having to defend government policies over which it had no authority in the first place.

The union has been a powerful advocate for the re-nationalisation of the railways, spreading its message in high profile campaigns and intensive lobbying. Despite being ejected by New Labour the union's arguments for re-nationalisation have won the day in the Labour Party as a whole. Ironically, in September 2004 at the first Labour Party conference held after RMT disaffiliation, delegates overwhelmingly passed a resolution backing re-nationalisation of rail, only to see the party hierarchy ignore the conference when it drew up the party manifesto. A similar motion easily passed the TUC conference the same year. In the run up to the 2005 general election the union launched a 'Rail Against Privatisation' mobile demonstration of 25 RMT activists who travelled from Glasgow to London, marching through the centres of twelve major cities, and spreading the message to tens of thousands of people. According to analysis of the RAP campaign by the Press Association, coverage of the mobile demonstration reached some 15 million people. The Rail Against Privatisation mobile demo was the most visible of a plethora of initiatives on re-nationalisation. The RMT parliamentary group was pivotal in keeping the issue alive in parliament, succeeding in getting over a hundred MPs to sign an early day motion in favour of re-nationalisation.

Developments on the railways have done nothing to dampen the ardour of calls for public ownership, nor stilled the outrage at the government's failure to take the opportunities for re-nationalisation provided since the collapse of Railtrack. Network Rail took over rail maintenance from the hapless Jarvis after the Hatfield accident. Since then other maintenance contracts have been taken back 'in house' by Network Rail. Freed from the constraints of commercial contracts and the blame culture which accompanied it, track maintenance work became more productive, staff morale went up. Delays caused by infrastructure failures have dropped by between 36 and 50 per cent. The government failed to extend this partial re-nationalisation of the network, though the opportunity was there. Rather than re-nationalise when the opportunity has arisen, as in the case of South East Trains, the franchise for which was taken back from Connex and is now being re-tendered, the government has chosen the route of re-privatisation. Meanwhile evidence continues to grow of the benefits of returning the railways to public ownership. Just before the 2005 general election the independent think tank Catalyst issued a report that demonstrated that re-nationalisation could save some £500 million per year. Public opinion polls have consistently shown widespread support for public ownership. The folly of privatisation is plain for all to see. The union's case for a publicly owned, publicly accountable railway has been won in the court of public opinion; it is only adherence to neo-liberal dogma by the government that prevents the disaster of privatisation from being ended.

The union has also been instrumental in the creation of a broad consensus for the repeal of much of the hated anti-trade union legislation of the 1980s. In the wake of the scandalous treatment of striking catering staff by the airline contractor Gate Gourmet in the summer of 2005, the RMT has assisted in creating the groundswell within the labour movement for the enshrining of the basic rights of workers, taken away by the Thatcher and Blair governments. It is engaged with other unions in the United Campaign for the Repeal of Anti Trade Union Laws, which in the centenary of the Trade Disputes Act of 1906 seeks to introduce legislation which enshrines the right of workers to organise in law. The RMT group of MPs have helped to draft an early day motion for a trade union freedom bill, which aims to strengthen a worker's right to withdraw labour without being sacked. Over 150 MPs have signed the EDM.

> We draw our strength from the past. It goes right the way back. The debate among working people at the turn of the last century was that the only way you are going to solve problems is through unity. When the first meeting of the ASRS was convened at the Winchester Arms in Southwark, Tom Hughes, the Liberal MP, got up and said 'look at your conditions, the awful situation you find yourselves in. There is only one way forward and I implore you to take it: that is to bury your sectionalist difference and unite into one industrial union'. From that meeting workers built themselves up with the understanding that the whole object of the union was to show solidarity with one another, and to develop a collective approach on every issue to employers. We have revived that along the way by trying to make industrial trade unionism a reality.
>
> Geoff Revell

The union's recent successes no doubt owe much to its organisational agility and willingness to use industrial action where necessary to face off intransigent employers. But the revival of industrial trade unionism within the RMT goes beyond mere tactics. The RMT has succeeded because its membership has been intensely conscious of its own history. The union's roots in the syndicalist period of 'all industry' trade unionism has given the RMT an identity as a specialist national union which organises across the transport sector.

The unique internal democratic structure of the union, in which executive members stand for regular elections and then go 'back on the tools' after their time in office, and in which the annual conference acts as the union's parliament, helps to create a culture of energetic

Within our union we don't differentiate between members. The relationship with the member and their employer is secondary to that fact. That's about pay and conditions. But within the RMT it doesn't matter what job anybody does, it's our union. That makes people proud of our organisation. They then are more willing to take on the bosses. As long as the union uses its resources to back people up in struggle, instead of acting as a policeman, we remain as one. The railways and the shipping lines and the bus companies may be split up but we are not. The union is not the centre, the union is everywhere in Britain, from John 'O Groats to Lands End.

Geoff Revell

democratic engagement that has enabled the RMT to rebuild itself in the aftermath of the battles of the 1980s and 1990s. Its membership have kept alive a tradition of workplace activism and resistance to exploitation which has, from the days of sail and steam, made the union what it is today. The union is also unashamedly socialist in its traditions and aspirations. It is proud of its role in the history of the wider trade union movement, in the creation of the Labour Party, and in the struggle for social justice in modern Britain. Some may see this commitment as utopian and anachronistic. But in a world wracked by new wars, scarred by poverty, exploitation and ethnic and religious violence, the historical values of the trade union movement, of a shared aspiration and commitment to building a society based on a human commonwealth are surely needed now more than ever. Whatever the future holds one thing is clear: the RMT will continue to fulfil its historic role within the trade union movement as a collective and class conscious voice for all transport workers. No matter what efforts lie ahead, an awareness of the legacy of past struggles, and of the solidarity and comradeship they engendered, will see the union through and give hope and inspiration to others.

# Bibliography

Alcock, G.W., *Fifty Years of Railway Trade Unionism* (London: Co-Operative Printing Society Ltd, 1922)

Anderson, P. and Mann, N., *Safety First: the Making of New Labour* (London: Granta Books, 1997)

Bagwell, Phillip, 'Early Attempts at National Organization of the Railwaymen 1865–67', *Journal of Transport History*, 3:2 (1957), 94–102

—— *The Railwaymen: the History of the National Union of Railwaymen*, 2 volumes (London: George Allen & Unwin, 1963 & 1982)

—— 'The Triple Alliance', in Asa Briggs and John Saville (eds), *Essays in Labour History, 1886–1923* (London: Macmillan Press, 1971), pp. 96–128

—— *The Transport Crisis in Britain* (Nottingham: Spokesman, 1996)

Crompton, G.W., '"Some Good Men, Some Doubtful Men": the Role of the Railway Volunteers in the General Strike', *Journal of Transport History* (September 1988), 126–48

Dodds, Andrew, *Almost* (London: Minerva Press, 2001)

Freeman, R. and Shaw, J., *All Change: British Rail Privatisation* (London: McGraw-Hill, 2000)

Frost, Diane (ed.), *Ethnic Labour and British Imperial Trade: a History of Ethnic Seafarers in the UK* (London: Cass, 1995)

Gourvish, T.R., *British Rail 1948–1973: a Business History* (Cambridge: Cambridge University Press, 1986)

—— *British Rail, 1974–97: from Integration to Privatisation* (Oxford: Oxford University Press, 2002)

Gupta, P.S., 'Railways Trade Unionism in Britain, c.1880–1900', *Economic History Review*, 2nd ser., 19:1 (1966), 124–53

Henshaw, D., *The Great Railway Conspiracy* (London: Leading Edge, 1991)

Howell, David, '"I loved my union and my country": Jimmy Thomas and the Politics of Railway Trade Unionism', *20th Century British History*, 6 (1995), 145–73

—— *Respectable Radicals: Studies in the Politics of Railway Trade Unionism* (Aldershot: Ashgate Publishing, 1999)

Kennerley, Alston, 'The Seamen's Union, the National Maritime Board and Firemen: Labour Management in the British Mercantile Marine', *Northern Mariner*, 7:4 (1997), 15–28

Kiloh, Margaret, *A Fighting Union: An Oral History of SARHWU* (Johannesburg: Raven Press, 1999)

Knapp, J., 'The History of a Merger', *On the Move: Essays in Labour and Transport History Presented to Phillip Bagwell*, eds C. Wrigley and J. Shepherd (London: Hambledon & London, 1991), 252–6

Lane, T., *Grey Dawn Breaking: British Seafarers in the Late Twentieth Century* (Manchester: Manchester University Press, 1986)

Marsh, A. and Ryan, V., *The Seamen: a History of the National Union of Seamen, 1887–1987* (Oxford: Oxford University Press, 1987)

McCord, Norman, 'Taff Vale Revisited', *History*, 78 (1993), 243–60

McKenna, F., *The Railway Workers, 1870–1970* (London: Faber & Faber, 1980)

McKillop, N., *The Lighted Flame: a History of ASLEF* (London: Thomas Nelson & Sons, 1930)

Minkin, Lewis, *The Contentious Alliance: Trade Unions and the Labour Party* (Edinburgh: Edinburgh University Press, 1991)

Murphy, Brian, *ASLEF 1880–1980: a Hundred Years of the Locomen's Trade Union* (London: Associated Society of Locomotive Engineers and Firemen, 1980)

Murray, A., *Off the Rails: Britain's Great Rail Crisis – Cause, Consequences and Cure* (London: Verso, 2001)

Nash, B., 'Labour Law and the State: the Crises of the Unions in the 1980s', Unpublished PhD thesis, Virginia Polytechnic Institute, 2000

Rowe, D.J., 'A Trade Union of the North East Coast Seamen in 1825', *Economic History Review*, 2nd ser., 25 (1972), 81–98

Thorpe, Keir, 'The "Juggernaut Method": the 1966 State of Emergency and the Wilson Government's Response to the Seamen's Strike', *20th Century British History*, 12:4 (2001), 461–85

Tupper, Edward, *Seamen's Torch: the Life of Captain Edward Tupper* (London: Hutchinson, 1938)

Vaughan, A., *Railwaymen, Politics and Money: the Great Age of Railways in Britain* (London: John Murray, 1997)

Wallace, M., *Single or Return? The History of the Transport Salaried Staffs' Association* (London: Transport Salaried Staffs' Association, 1996)

Weighell, Sidney, *On the Rails* (London: Orbus, 1983)

—— *A Hundred Years of Railway Weighells* (London: Robson, 1984)

Wojtczak, H., *Railwaywomen: Exploitation, Betrayal and Triumph in the Workplace* (Hastings: Hastings Press, 2005)

Wolmar, C., *Broken Rails: How Privatisation Wrecked Britain's Railways* (London: Aurum Press, 2001)

—— *Down the Tubes: the Battle for London's Underground* (London: Aurum Press, 2002)

# Index

*Compiled by Sue Carlton*